The Princeton Review

Grammar Smart Junior

Good Grammar Made Easy

BOOKS IN THE PRINCETON REVIEW SERIES

Cracking the ACT
Cracking the ACT with Sample Tests on CD-ROM
Cracking the CLEP (College-Level Examination Program)
Cracking the GED
Cracking the GMAT
Cracking the GMAT with Sample Tests on Computer Disk
Cracking the GRE
Cracking the GRE with Sample Tests on Computer Disk
Cracking the GRE Biology Subject Test
Cracking the GRE Literature in English Subject Test
Cracking the GRE Psychology Subject Test
Cracking the LSAT
Cracking the LSAT with Sample Tests on Computer Disk
Cracking the LSAT with Sample Tests on CD-ROM
Cracking the MAT (Miller Analogies Test)
Cracking the NTE with Audio CD-ROM
Cracking the SAT and PSAT
Cracking the SAT and PSAT with Sample Tests on
    Computer Disk
Cracking the SAT and PSAT with Sample Tests on CD-ROM
Cracking the SAT II: Biology Subject Test
Cracking the SAT II: Chemistry Subject Test
Cracking the SAT II: English Subject Tests
Cracking the SAT II: French Subject Test
Cracking the SAT II: History Subject Tests
Cracking the SAT II: Math Subject Tests
Cracking the SAT II: Physics Subject Test
Cracking the SAT II: Spanish Subject Test
Cracking the TOEFL with Audiocassette
Flowers & Silver MCAT
Flowers Annotated MCAT
Flowers Annotated MCATs with Sample Tests on
    Computer Disk
Flowers Annotated MCATs with Sample Tests on CD-ROM

Culturescope Grade School Edition
Culturescope High School Edition
Culturescope College Edition

LSAT/GRE Analytic Workout
SAT Math Workout
SAT Verbal Workout

All U Can Eat
Don't Be a Chump!
How to Survive Without Your Parents' Money
Speak Now!
Trashproof Resumes

Biology Smart
Grammar Smart
Math Smart
Reading Smart
Study Smart
Word Smart: Building an Educated Vocabulary
Word Smart II: How to Build a More Educated Vocabulary
Word Smart Executive
Word Smart Genius
Writing Smart

American History Smart Junior
Astronomy Smart Junior
Geography Smart Junior
Grammar Smart Junior
Math Smart Junior
Word Smart Junior
Writing Smart Junior

Business School Companion
College Companion
Law School Companion
Medical School Companion

Student Advantage Guide to College Admissions
Student Advantage Guide to the Best 310 Colleges
Student Advantage Guide to America's Top Internships
Student Advantage Guide to Business Schools
Student Advantage Guide to Law Schools
Student Advantage Guide to Medical Schools
Student Advantage Guide to Paying for College
Student Advantage Guide to Summer
Student Advantage Guide to Visiting College Campuses
Student Advantage Guide: Help Yourself
Student Advantage Guide: The Complete Book of Colleges
Student Advantage Guide: The Internship Bible
Hillel Guide to Jewish Life on Campus
International Students' Guide to the United States
The Princeton Review Guide to Your Career

Also available on cassette from Living Language
Grammar Smart
Word Smart
Word Smart II

The Princeton Review

Grammar
Smart
Junior

Good Grammar Made Easy

by Liz Buffa

Random House, Inc., New York

Copyright © 1995 by Princeton Review Publishing, L.L.C.
Illustrations copyright © 1995 by Jeff Moores.

Library of Congress Cataloging-in-Publication Data

Buffa, Liz
    The Princeton Review grammar smart junior: an introduction
to proper usage/Liz Buffa.—1st ed.
        p. cm.
    Summary: An introduction to over 650 words students should
know by the time they enter high school. Uses stories to
present words in context and has quizzes for reinforcement.

    ISBN 0-679-76212-4

    1. English language—Grammar—Juvenile Literature. 2. English
language—Usage—Juvenile Literature. I. Princeton Review
(Firm) II. Title
LB1576.B886   1995
372.6'1—dc20   95-8500
                                                        CIP
                                                         AC

Manufactured in the United States of America on recycled paper.
9 8 7 6 5 4

ACKNOWLEDGMENTS

The author would like to thank the following for their invaluable contributions: Michael Freedman, Marcia Lerner, Diane Fagiola, and Marissa La Magna for their emotional support. Special thanks to Bronwyn Collie, Lee Elliott, Chris Kensler and Meher Khambata, Illeny Maaza, and Christopher D. Scott for their wonderful work in putting the book together.

And thanks of course to Dominick, David, and Paul, for their patience and proofreading.

CONTENTS

Introduction

WHY SHOULD I LEARN ABOUT GRAMMAR?

Some of you are better at fashion, some of you are better at reading, and some of you are better at making great lay-ups on the basketball court. Whatever your skills are, and whatever it is you like, you most certainly have to talk to people and write from time to time. You may be able to ignore basketball, but you can't ignore the English language. Communication is important, and using proper grammar is also important, for two reasons: *to be clear*, and *to sound educated*. Huh?

Let us explain. Many of the grammar rules you will encounter are there to make your life *easier*. Remember: you need to communicate with people, right? Well, let's say you write this in a paper:

> I told Maria that I like Smashing Pumpkins'
> new CD more than her.

Now, did you just insult your friend by saying that you like a CD more than you like her? Or, did you just say that you like this particular CD more than she likes it? Well, to be honest, according to the rules of grammar, you told her that you like this CD more than you like her, and that's probably not what you meant.

That's the first thing grammar helps you do—if you use your words carefully and correctly, you will avoid misunderstandings.

Now, About the Sounding Educated Part . . .

Sure, we want you to speak and write perfectly all the time because there is beauty in doing so. But, if beauty alone is not enough incentive for you, how about things like getting good grades and good jobs? You know the unfortunate truth: no matter how wonderful your thoughts are, if they're written with lots of grammatical errors, you won't get a good grade. And, no matter how wonderful a person you are, if you go into a job interview years from now and say:

> "I just know I done good on that test you gave me, sir!"

well, you won't be getting that job. So, knowing proper grammar is important for many reasons.

Well, What's This Book About?

We want to teach you good grammar and make it incredibly *clear*, *easy* and, most of all, *interesting*. We don't necessarily expect you to read this book from cover to cover; some of you will just use it for reference when you have a specific question. That's fine. We'll remind you from time to time about which rules are *really* important rules that you should always follow no matter what, and which rules are the sort that only English teachers will give you a hard time about.

But I Hate Grammar . . .

Okay, it's not your fault. Grammar can be boring, and it doesn't make much sense when you are asked to speak one way, but often hear English spoken in a completely different way. That's confusing. When you watch TV, read magazines, look at advertisements, listen to music, you are constantly exposed to bad grammar.

Now, don't get us wrong. We have nothing against bad grammar in things like music or advertising. Sometimes using the wrong word sounds better when you're writing lyrics to a song or jingle. But you aren't a famous rock star (yet). We're going to help you learn the difference between good and bad grammar and help you do better on tests and papers, and with your classes, because in those situations, bad grammar is definitely not okay.

TESTS?

Sure, tests. Even if you haven't had them yet, pretty soon you'll be called upon to answer questions about grammar: your teacher will ask you what a dependent clause is, or to identify the errors in a poorly written sentence. Both these things will be simple if you start now by getting an ear for good grammar. What does that mean? If you have an ear for music, you might recognize immediately if a song is by Gloria Estefan or Green Day. If you have an ear for good grammar, you will recognize when something just doesn't sound right.

BUT WAIT A MINUTE . . . MY COMPUTER HAS A GRAMMAR CHECK AND A SPELL CHECK!

Okay, sure, you caught us. There is, in fact, a grammar check and a spell check on many computer programs. And some silly people now believe that there will be no reason in the future for kids to learn grammar and spelling, since it will simply be a matter of hitting a key and letting the computer change your wonderful, yet grammatically incorrect thoughts into perfect, sparkling English. Well, we hate to break this to you, but *the grammar and spelling programs don't always work*.

Really. Would we lie to you? Okay, spell checkers work pretty well. They'll pick up some misspellings. But, first, you have to spell a word *sort of* right for a spell checker to correct it. If you're *way* off, it won't know what word you're talking about. (It is only a machine, after all.) And, it won't pick up misspellings in which you turn one word into another. For example if you spell *you're* as *your*. Both are correctly spelled words, and the spell checker only picks out words that don't appear in its dictionary.

And those grammar checks? Forget them. As of now, they are pretty much useless. If you tried to use a grammar check on a paper, chances are you'd be more lost after you were done than before you started.

So, sorry. Just be grateful we're here to help you.

How to Use this Book

This book is arranged so that it will be easy to follow and fun to read. You can, if you want, read it through a little at a time and test yourself with the quizzes that follow each topic. They are there for you to figure out if you get the idea. You don't have to get every question right to feel good about yourself. If you get most of the questions right on the quizzes, you're doing well. While you're doing that, you can follow the story of a group of friends who were just hanging out one day when they found their ticket to adventureland!

Those of you who open the book only to find an answer to a specific question should appreciate that we go in order, from basic definitions to more detailed points of grammar to common errors and tips. You may find yourself reading a little bit ahead just to see how things really work in this complicated machine we call grammar. It's not so bad—and speaking and writing well are your rewards.

Chapter 1
The Names
of Things

To learn about grammar, you have to start by learning the names of things. The parts of speech are the pieces you use to put sentences and paragraphs together. To put them together properly, you need to know what each piece is called and what role it plays.

So, what's the point? Well, we won't fool you. Chances are good that, unless you become a contestant on "Jeopardy" in your adult life, you won't be called upon regularly to name the parts of speech. So, do we really care if you can name the parts of speech with your eyes closed? No, not really. We are defining these terms so that you will understand what we are talking about throughout the book. And, chances are that, as a student, you will need to know these terms when your teacher gives you one of those nasty little quizzes that teachers so love to give.

If you play hockey, you don't need to know the name of a squeeze play to make one, right? And, you don't need to know the name of a reflexive pronoun to use one properly. But, if you look blankly up at your coach when he advises you to make one of those great squeeze plays, he may think, "Hey, I'm not sure if this kid really knows how to play hockey."

Okay, so words are put into eight different categories depending on the roles they play in sentences. The eight parts of speech are:

nouns

pronouns

verbs

adjectives

adverbs

prepositions

conjunctions

interjections

The easiest way to find out what part of speech a word is, if you're really confused, is to look the word up in a dictionary. A dictionary definition will include information about what part of speech a word is. For example:

fly, n.; pl. flies. 1. a housefly; any of a group of insects with two transparent wings, including the housefly and the Mayfly. 2. a device made of feathers, silk, etc., to resemble an insect, used in fishing as a bait.

Now, as you can see, this is the definition of *fly* that means an insect or fishing lure. That little *n.* after the word tells you that *fly* is a noun, and the *pl.* tells you that the plural of *fly* is *flies*. It gives you two definitions. (The first is always the most common use of the word.)

But, there's another definition of fly that means something completely different:

fly, v.; flew, pt.; flown, pp. 1. to move through the air, with wings, as a bird flies, or by airplane. 2. to operate an airplane. 3. to float in the air, as a kite or flag does.

This definition of fly indicates that *fly* can also be a verb. It also gives you some of the different tenses of the verb.

We'll get into those later, in chapter 3. But for now, you should know that a word might only, and always, be one part of speech, or it may be different parts of speech depending on the way it is used in a sentence.

NOUNS

A noun is a person, place, thing, or idea.

Person: Pierre, Juanita, Mary, friend, mom

Place: school, home, McDonald's

Thing: cat, calendar, stereo, CD

Idea: truth, justice, the American way

There are two general categories of nouns: common nouns and proper nouns.

A common noun is a word that names *any* person, place, or thing. A proper noun names a *specific* person, place, or thing. Compare the two:

Common noun	Proper noun
girl	Maria
teacher	Mr. Escobar
city	Shakey Heights
state	Alaska
college	Michigan State

What do you notice about common nouns and proper nouns? Proper nouns are always capitalized and common nouns are not (unless they begin a sentence, of course).

In the following paragraph, the nouns are in italics.

> *Jem* stayed moody and silent for a *week*. As *Atticus* had once advised me to do, I tried to climb into *Jem's skin* and walk around in it: if I had not gone to the *Radley Place* at two in the *morning*, my *funeral* would have been held the next *afternoon*. So I left *Jem* alone and tried not to bother him.
>
> from *To Kill A Mockingbird*, Harper Lee

✍ QUIZ #1 ✍
What's this Ticket?

Underline the common nouns and circle the proper nouns in the following passage.

It was a hot day around the old clubhouse. Sondra, Barnaby, Babette, Taylor, Bridget, and Jennifer had been hanging around watching television most of that week—it seemed too hot to do anything else.

"Man, what I wouldn't do to spend a week on Gilligan's Island," said Barnaby. "First of all, I wouldn't mind meeting the Professor, and secondly, it would be nice and cool there."

"Forget Gilligan's Island," answered Jennifer. "Give me Melrose Place any day. I'd love to hang with Amanda, meet Jake, bum around with that whole gang. Their lives seem so exciting."

"You guys are weird," said Taylor, dreamily. "Give me a nice happy family like the Brady Bunch. Now there are some fun people I'd like to spend a week with."

"What's this ticket on the floor?" asked Bridget. "I've never seen anything like it before."

PRONOUNS

Okay, now that you know what a noun is, you'll recognize pronouns. Pronouns are used as stand-ins for nouns—sort of like noun stunt players. Think of how horrible and awkward your sentences would sound without pronouns to stand in for nouns every now and then. You get to say, for example:

> Marcia told John that she liked his story better than she liked hers.

Instead of:

> Marcia told John that Marcia liked John's story better than Marcia liked Marcia's story.

Obviously, pronouns make your sentences a little smoother. Using them means you don't have to repeat the nouns over and over again, when we all know to what noun you're referring. The italicized words in the following paragraph are pronouns.

> *We* lived on the main residential street in town—Atticus, Jem and *I*, plus Calpurnia our cook. Jem and *I* found *our* father satisfactory: *he* played with *us*, read to *us*, and treated *us* with courteous detachment.
>
> from *To Kill a Mockingbird*, Harper Lee

✍ QUIZ #2 ✍
A Ticket to Adventure

Underline the pronouns in the following passage.

"It says, 'This is your ticket to adventure. If you hold tightly onto it, you will be transported to the place of your dreams. To escape from your adventure, say the words *anna banana*,'" said Jennifer.

"That's strange. What do you suppose it means?" wondered Babette.

"I suppose that it means exactly what it says. Where would we like to go?" answered Barnaby, logical as usual.

"Me, I would like to go to Melrose Place," laughed Jennifer, picking up the ticket.

"That seems like a weird place to me," said Taylor.

But it was too late. The clubhouse began to rattle. They all held onto the nearest piece of furniture. Before you could say "Sydney," they were off.

VERBS

A verb is a word that expresses an action or a state of being. A verb is one of the most important words in a sentence— you cannot express a complete thought without a verb.

The action may be:

Physical: I *ran* through the field.

Josh *played* football on Saturday morning.

Mental: I *thought* you'd be here.

Paul *felt* sick.

As a "state of being," a verb expresses what something is, or its condition, rather than a real action.

State of being: Jane *is* happy.

Jordan *was* successful.

In the following paragraph, all the verbs are in italics.

Lennie *went* behind the tree and *brought* out a litter of dried leaves and twigs. He *threw* them in a heap on the old ash pile and *went* back for more and more. It *was* almost night now. A dove's wings *whistled* over the water. George *walked* to the fire pile and *lighted* the dry leaves. The flame *crackled* up among the twigs and *fell* to work. George *undid* his bundle and *brought* out three cans of beans.

from *Of Mice and Men*, John Steinbeck

✍ QUIZ #3 ✍
Melrose Place, Here We Come!

Underline the verbs in the following passage.

Jennifer opened the door slowly. The pool glimmered in the mid-afternoon sun. Soon, she heard a familiar voice screech into the silence.

"What is this disgustingly ugly house doing in *my* pool?" yelled Amanda.

"Uh, we're not exactly sure ourselves," answered Jennifer. "Is this really Melrose Place?"

"You bet, sweetie," answered Amanda. "And if you don't hightail this broken down old clubhouse from our private pool, you will live to regret your visit here."

"Amanda, what is the problem?" Jake entered the scene.

"No problem, sweetie. Just a bunch of rude, noisy kids trespassing on our property. I'm sure they'll find a way out of here before you can wink an eye." Amanda turned on her heel, stomped into the apartment, and slammed the door behind her.

"Hmm, what do you think of Amanda now?" asked Sondra.

"Ugh," answered Jennifer. "*Anna banana.*"

ADJECTIVES

It would be a dreary world indeed without adjectives. As a matter of fact, it would just be a world, because there'd be no words like *dreary*. Now, you may have thought that nouns and pronouns and verbs were just okay, but adjectives, well, that's another story. In grammar and writing, the fun really starts when you get to *describe* things, and that's where adjectives come in. An adjective is a word that describes or modifies a noun. An adjective answers questions about a noun. For example:

Noun: Book—What kind of book is it?

It is a *red* book.

It is a *large* book.

Noun: House—Whose house is it?

It is *my* house.

Our house is down the street.

Noun: Computer—Which computer is it?

Which computer are you working on?

What computer did you sit at?

This computer is my favorite.

That computer is bad.

In the following paragraph, all the adjectives are in italics.

He stood frowning as the ring of *blue-white* fire flickered and danced; he even looked *cold*, with a *dark pinched* look round the bones of his face. "They bring in the *deep* cold," he said, half to himself. "The cold of the void, of *black* space . . ."

from *The Dark is Rising*, Susan Cooper

Just Sit Right Back and You'll Hear a Tale . . .

Underline the adjectives in the following passage.

The clubhouse may have been shabby, but it was sturdy enough to get them back home in a wink.

"Wow," said Jennifer, "this silver ticket really works! We should think hard about the next exciting place we'd like to go."

"We could go somewhere cool," offered Barnaby.

"Somewhere fun," said Babette.

"Somewhere exotic," said Taylor.

"Hmm, Melrose Place wasn't exotic enough for you?" asked a nervous Bridget. She snapped her cherry gum and blew an enormous bubble.

"No, let's try someplace new and different," answered Babette.

"Someplace where there are cool ocean breezes, perhaps?" asked Barnaby.

"Yeah, cool, fresh breezes. That sounds pretty nice." Taylor looked off into the steamy street.

"Maybe Gilligan's Island?" Barnaby grabbed the silver ticket and rubbed it.

ADVERBS

Adverbs are like the workhorses of describing words. While an adjective describes a noun, an adverb is a word that describes or modifies a verb, an adjective, or even another adverb. Adverbs answer questions about verbs, adjectives, or other adverbs. What does that mean? Here are some examples:

David *always* eats a lot.

Diane did well *enough* on her exam.

These answer the question "how?" The first adverb describes the verb "eats" and tells you *how much* David eats. The second adverb describes the adverb "well" and tells you *how well* Diane did.

He will be here *later*.

Mr. Bradley will arrive *soon*.

These answer the question "when?" The first adverb describes the verb "will be" and tells you *when* he will be here. The second adverb describes the verb "will arrive" and tells you *when* Mr. Bradley will arrive.

Evan ran *behind*.

Mary Ann looked *there*.

These adverbs answer the question "where?" The first one describes the verb "ran" and tells you *where* Evan ran. The second one describes the verb "looked" and tells you *where* Mary Ann looked.

I *really, really* want to go to the movies.

Peter will *actually* go along with me.

These adverbs are used for emphasis. The first one emphasizes the verb "want." The second emphasizes the verb "will go."

Dominick runs *swiftly*.

Dan sings *happily*.

These are the most common adverbs. They end in -ly and answer the question "how?" How does Dominick run? *Swiftly*. How does Dan sing? *Happily*.

Many adverbs end in *-ly*, but, as you can see, many do not.

✍ QUIZ #5 ✍
The Professor and Barnaby

Underline the adverbs in the following passage.

"Gilligan!" yelled Mary Ann. She ran breathlessly up the beach and into the woods.

The kids were perched clumsily in the nearest coconut tree.

"What's the matter Mary Ann? You seem very upset." Gilligan ran quickly to her.

"No, it's just that I heard something—a very funny kind of crash. I'm a little scared, Gilligan. Let's go get the Professor." "The Professor!" whispered Barnaby excitedly. "I have always wanted to meet him. One of the great minds of sitcom land."

"Sure, if he's so very smart, how come he never got them off this stupid island?" Bridget snapped her gum furiously.

"Sssh, Bridget, here he comes!" Barnaby pointed at the figure moving slowly through the clump of trees.

"Professor, we're really stuck. Here! Up in this tree!" called Barnaby.

"My, my, how did you kids get stuck up in a coconut tree?" pondered the Professor. "And who are you, anyway? How can we be sure that you aren't a bunch of spies, sent here by some of our enemies?"

"Spies? Professor, I am your very biggest fan," cried Barnaby.

"Oh, really?" asked the Professor. "And how is it that you know my name?"

PREPOSITIONS

A preposition is a word that shows how a noun or pronoun is related to another word in a sentence. It gives the noun's relation in place, direction, or time. For example:

Place: Alice was *at* her desk.

She was *behind* her friend.

At and *behind* place Alice in relation to her friend and her desk.

Direction: I was going *to* the movies.

Martha came *from* the pizza parlor.

To and *from* give you the directions Martha and I are going in relation to something else (here, the movies and the pizza parlor).

Time: I'd rather go skiing *in* February.

Melanie will be home *at* 3:00 p.m.

In and *at* both connect the nouns to time—February and 3:00 p.m.

Here are some examples of prepositions:

Place: around, through, over, above, in, after, at, behind, under

Direction: from, to, away, after, into

Time: before, by, at, after, on, in

✍ QUIZ #6 ✐
Court Martial on Gilligan's Island

Circle the prepositions in the following passage.

Once in the hut, the kids began to panic. "How did we get ourselves into this?" asked Taylor.

"Don't worry—I'll get us out of this trouble." Barnaby was confident. "I can reason with the Professor."

"Okay, kids, we don't know who you are, but we suspect you are a bunch of spies. How else would you all know our names?" said the Skipper pacing around the room as he spoke.

"I can prove we're not spies!" cried Babette. "I don't know anything about this stupid show! I only watch *Beverly Hills 90210.*"

"A likely story!" answered Ginger. "I've been to Beverly Hills, of course, and I'm sure it would be very boring to just sit and watch it all day long. Only a spy would do that! They're trying to learn all of our customs."

"Let's feed them to the crocodiles!" yelled Mary Ann.

"No, let's send them out on a raft!" countered the Professor.

"Forget it!" Barnaby rolled his eyes. *"Anna banana."*

CONJUNCTIONS

A conjunction is a joining word. You might say:

> Juanita went to school. She took a test.

But, you could make those two sentences into one with a conjunction:

> Juanita went to school and she took a test.

Or even:

> Juanita went to school and took a test.

Conjunctions are pretty easy to spot. They join two or more things together in a sentence. Some conjunctions work alone:

> If you go to the store, take the dog *and* the cat.
>
> I wanted to bring our goldfish, *but* my mother said no.
>
> If you bring the goldfish *or* the snails, they might die.
>
> *Although* I like snails, I prefer goldfish.

(Notice with that last example that conjunctions don't always come between the things they join. "Although" joins the clauses *I like snails* and *I prefer goldfish.*)

Some conjunctions work in pairs:

> *Neither* Ollie *nor* Stan would have eaten that goldfish!

> *Either* goldfish *or* snails are delicious when cooked with garlic.

> *Not only* garlic, *but also* onions, are necessary when preparing such delicacies!

✐ QUIZ #7 ✐
Wilma!

Underline the conjunctions in the following passage.

"Ugh," Barnaby rolled his eyes as they landed back at home. "Neither Melrose Place nor Gilligan's Island was at all what I'd imagined."

"Maybe we'd better forget all about this ticket and traveling for today." Bridget snapped her gum.

"Not only are you guys boring, but you also lack imagination," Sondra said. "Let's go someplace, I don't know, unreal. How about Bedrock?"

"Where?" asked Taylor. He had never heard of Melrose Place or Bedrock. This day was beginning to tire him out.

"You know—Fred, Wilma, Betty, and Barney. Bedrock!"

"Barney? You mean that large purple dinosaur. I don't think so!" Babette wrinkled her nose and threw her hands up in disgust.

"Not Barney the purple dinosaur, Babette, Barney from the cartoon *The Flintstones*. C'mon, either you give me that ticket or I'll never speak to you again."

"Here—do what you want—I give up." Barnaby tossed the ticket at Sondra's feet.

"Wilma—I always wanted to meet you and Betty." Sondra rubbed the ticket. The walls of the clubhouse began to shimmer. The kids felt weird and wobbly. They were turning into cartoon characters!

INTERJECTIONS

Hey! Yo! Cool! It's interjection time. Interjections are easy and fun and have no real rules, which makes them especially great. An interjection is a word that stands alone which you can add for emphasis.

Wow! What a great new haircut.

Yecch! You look stupid.

Ha! What do you know about it?

Not all interjections are followed by exclamation points. Sometimes, words that act like an introduction are considered interjections. For example:

Really, you should cut your hair.

Yes, you are right.

✍ QUIZ #8 ✐
We Forgot About the Dinosaurs

Ha! Find the interjections! Underline them!

"Heh! Barney," called Fred. "Check this out."

"What is it Fred?" Barney leaned over the stone fence between their houses. "Yikes! What's that, Fred?"

"I'm not sure Barn—it looks like some kind of strange wooden house. Who ever heard of a wooden house?"

The kids nervously peered out the window.

"Cool! We're cartoons. Look, Sondra, there's Fred and Barney. They're pointing at us. Wave."

"Heh, you kids. What are you doing in our tree? Wilma! Call the Rock Police!"

"Oh!" Wilma walked out into the yard. "What's going on here, Fred?"

Dino came bounding into the yard. "Yip, yip!" He jumped up at the base of the tree, clawing furiously at the bottom of the clubhouse.

"They don't seem very friendly, either," Sondra shook her head.

"Oh, well, *anna banana*."

Party On with Parts of Speech

Okay, you've finished the parts of speech. Now you can play the parts of speech games. You'll need a friend or two. Ask each person to call out a word that is the part of speech required in each blank. Don't tell your friends the title or the subject of the story. The more creative the words, the funnier the result. Read the story out loud once the blanks are all filled in.

✍ PARTS OF SPEECH GAME #1 ✍
Candy Warning

Warning: Candy can be Hazardous to your Health

Washington, DC: The National Health Department released a (noun)_____ warning young (plural noun)_____ about the dangers of (verb ending in -ing)_____ candy.

"Many people don't realize that candy contains (noun)_____," warned a senior official at the Department.

"If you eat (adjective)_____ candy three or more times a (noun)_____, you will jeopardize your chances of growing up (adjective)_____."

"(interjection)_____!" proclaimed a group of (nouns)_____. "We love to (verb)_____ candy. We _____(verb) it almost once a day!"

To minimize the danger, officials advise that you (verb)_____ your candy (adverb)_____ and (verb)_____ immediately (preposition) _____ your house.

✍ PARTS OF SPEECH GAME #2 ✍
School Survival Guide

If you want to make it through a (noun)_____ at school, you should always remember to (verb) _____ your teachers. If you (verb)_____ your (adjective)_____ teachers, you can expect to (verb) _____ every single time.

How do you (verb)_____ time and time again? (Interjection) _____ ! Call your teacher a (noun) _____ and (singular pronoun) _____ will really (verb) _____ your effort. Another sure-fire way to (verb) _____ your (adjective)_____ teacher is to (adverb) _____ (verb) _____ that teacher in front of the whole (group noun) _____.

✍ PARTS OF SPEECH GAME #3 ✍
A Trip to the Moon

Are you interested in (verb ending in -ing) _____ to the moon? Well, you will need a/an (adjective) _____ (noun) _____ and your favorite (noun) _____. Take these things and (verb) _____ them together in your best (noun) _____.

"(Interjection) _____!" you may say, "Is that all I need to (verb) _____ to the moon?"

"(Interjection) _____!" is what I say to you. All it takes is a couple of (nouns) _____ and a few very (adjective) _____ (nouns) _____ and soon you'll be (adverb) _____ on your way! Bon voyage!

Review

There are *eight* parts of speech. Give a quick definition and an example of each one. The answers are on pages 118-119.

1. _____

_____

_____

2. _____

_____

_____

3. _____

_____

_____

4. _____

_____

_____

5. _____

_____

_____

6. _____

_____

_____

7. _____

_____

_____

8. _____

_____

_____

Now that you've named the parts of speech, can you identify them in a sentence? In each of the following sentences write, below each word, what part of speech it is. Use *N* for noun, *P* for pronoun, *V* for verb, *ADJ* for adjective, *ADV* for adverb, *PR* for preposition, *C* for conjunction and *I* for interjection. This is tricky, but don't get discouraged.

1. Rose and Lionel went to the store.

   _____

2. They wanted to buy some comic books with their money.

   _____

3. "Yikes!" cried Lionel. "*X-Men* is on sale."

   _____

4. "I love *X-Men*, but *Spawn* is a great comic, too."

   _____

5. "*Spawn* and *X-Men* are both excellent."

   _____

Chapter 2
The Sentence

Okay, now that you know the parts of speech, let's talk about how sentences are put together. The parts of speech play different roles in different sentences. There are two main parts of a sentence. They are: the **subject** and the **predicate**.

Now, why should you care about this? Well, that's simple: because there must be a subject and a predicate in a complete sentence. Look at the following examples.

Not a sentence: John and Mary

Not a sentence: Went to the store

A sentence: John and Mary went to the store.

But, do you always speak in complete sentences? No way! There are plenty of times when, for creative purposes, you may use only a fragment, or a piece of a sentence, to make your point. But, if you are using fragments when you should be using full, complete sentences (in formal writing, for example), you will find yourself in hot water.

THE SUBJECT

If your friend asked you what the subject of the book you were reading was, you'd tell her what the book was about, right? Well, the subject of a sentence is simply what the sentence is about. The easiest way to find the subject of a sentence is to locate the verb, then ask yourself who or what is doing that action. For example, look at the sentence:

Bob ran in the race.

What is the verb? *Ran.* Who ran? Bob. *Bob* is the subject of the sentence.

Not all subjects come first in a sentence:

After running in the race, Eileen was exhausted.

What is the verb? *Was exhausted.* Who was exhausted? Eileen. *Eileen* is the subject of the sentence.

Some sentences have more than one subject. Check out this one:

While Mike was painting, Grace was working
on her paper.

There are two actions in this sentence—painting and writing. Who was painting? Mike. *Mike* is the subject of the first half of the sentence. Who was writing? Grace. *Grace* is the subject of the second half.

There is *always* a subject in a sentence. Sometimes, however, you don't hear or see the subject. These subjects are *implied.* What does it mean to imply something? It means that you don't say it straight out, but it's what you mean. Saying "I guess you didn't study for this exam," is a teacher's way of implying that you didn't do that well, right?

So what is an implied subject? Look at this example:

Drop dead!

This sentence is a complete thought. And how do you figure out the subject? Well, just as before, ask yourself these questions. What is the verb? *Drop.* Who is supposed to drop? Well, sorry, but you are. The subject here is you. In other words, the speaker is implying this:

You drop dead!

Sometimes, then, when a speaker is directing a comment right at someone, he won't say "you" but "you" is implied. Here are more examples of an implied subject:

> Get out of there.

> Don't eat that ice cream.

> Wait until 4:30.

✍ QUIZ #9 ✍
Subjects

Underline the subject in each of the following sentences.

1. Amanda stormed into the room.
2. "Get away from my boyfriend!"
3. "He is not your boyfriend!"
4. Amanda picked up a chair and threw it at Jennifer.
5. Without a moment's hesitation, Jennifer ran out of the room.

Sometimes there are words between the subject and the verb; don't let these throw you off. For example:

> Mary, the best student in class, was awarded the blue ribbon.

Who was awarded? Mary—so Mary is the subject. The phrase "the best student in class" describes Mary.

Now look at the following sentence:

> One of the boys was going to give the speech.

This is a little trickier. Who is giving the speech? Not boys, but *one of the boys*. *One of the boys* is the subject. When you are looking for the subject, try to ignore the words that are describing it. Look for the verb and ask yourself who or what is performing the action.

✍ QUIZ #10 ✎
Beverly Hills, Here We Come!

In the following passage, underline each verb and circle the subject that goes with it.

Thump. The clubhouse landed back in Babette's yard.

"I am glad we're not cartoons any longer," Sondra felt her arms and legs, "I sure didn't like that feeling."

"Well, we have had a very exciting day so far, but we have been somewhat unlucky in our choices," Barnaby said.

"Listen, guys, you just don't know how to pick nice, happy, fun places." Bridget blew a huge bubble, and was lifted off the ground a few inches. "Why don't we go and visit the Beverly Hillbillies? Now, there is a bunch of friendly, down home folk. Jethro is dreamy. Elly Mae is sweet. Give me that ticket."

Bridget rubbed the ticket while humming the theme song to *The Beverly Hillbillies*. The clubhouse began to shake once more.

THE PREDICATE

What is the predicate? Well, the short answer to that question is "everything that is not the subject." The easiest way to find the predicate is to do your subject search (Where's the verb? Who or what is the verb talking about?), then the verb and all the rest of the sentence is the predicate. Take a look at some simple examples:

Subject	Predicate
Jake	was a man.
He	was nice to everybody.

Now, you must not think, from our simple examples, that the subject always comes first, and that the predicate always comes second. That's probably the easiest way to write sentences, but it would be boring if all sentences were constructed this way.

Sentences should be different from each other in good writing. That means that some sentences will be long and intricate, and others will be short and simple. Varying sentences in this way makes a piece of writing far more interesting to read. So, let's look at a more complicated sentence and find the subject and the predicate:

> Throughout the history of the school, thousands of kids have walked these halls.

The verb of this sentence is *have walked*. Who or what *have walked*? Thousands of kids. So, *thousands of kids* is the subject of the sentence. And what is the predicate? *Throughout the history of the school . . . have walked these halls.*

Now take a look at this one:

> There are a million reasons to eat candy.

First of all, remember that "there" is never the subject of a sentence; if you see "there" at the beginning, the subject will probably follow the verb. So what is the verb? *Are.* There are *a million reasons*. *A million reasons* is the subject. Therefore, *There are . . . to eat candy* is the predicate.

✍ QUIZ #11 ✍

What's That in the Cement Pond?
or Granny's Got a Gun!

Underline the subject and put parentheses around the predicate in each of the following sentences.

The water began to bubble up around their feet. The clubhouse was barely floating.

"We've landed in another swimming pool!" Bridget wailed. "What are we going to do?"

"Well, we should probably get out of this clubhouse pronto," Barnaby suggested.

Jennifer peered out of the window. "I don't think that is a very good idea, Barnaby."

"Why would you say that, Jennifer? We happen to be sinking."

"Yeah, well I think I would rather drown." Jennifer pointed out of the window.

"Granny's got a gun!" Bridget yelled.

"What are you varmints doing in our ce-ment pond?" Granny aimed the gun straight at the clubhouse. "You can tell me or tell my gun!"

"*Anna banana*!" they all yelled at once.

Subject and Predicate Review

• Every sentence has a subject and a predicate.

• To find the subject:
  Locate the verb.
  Ask yourself "who or what is the verb talking about?"
  That "who or what" is the subject.

• The predicate is everything that is not the subject. The predicate may be a simple verb, or it may be the verb and all the extra things that are talking about the subject.

✍ QUIZ #12 ✍
Complete Sentences

Mark the complete sentences with an "S." Mark the fragments with an "F."

___ 1. Granny marched into the room.

___ 2. After looking at the wreckage, left to find Jed.

___ 3. Sniffling and crying in the corner.

___ 4. Elly Mae was a mess.

___ 5. Jethro couldn't help but notice what a mess Elly Mae was.

There are two more definitions you need to know before moving on to the more complicated points of grammar. These are phrases and clauses.

PHRASES

A phrase is a group of words that cannot stand alone as a sentence. The words in a phrase work together as a part of speech. For example, they may work together to name a person, place, thing, or idea. In this case the group of words would be called a **noun phrase**. The two most common phrases, however, are the **prepositional phrase** and the **verbal phrase**.

Prepositional Phrases

Remember prepositions? They're those little words that locate a noun in time, space, or direction. Prepositional phrases always begin with a preposition and end with a noun. For example:

> around the house
>
> *preposition   noun*
>
> through the door
>
> *preposition   noun*
>
> behind the wall
>
> *preposition   noun*

These are all prepositional phrases. Now, you have to decide what part of speech these phrases are acting as by looking at how they work in the sentence.

> The black cat was buried *behind the wall.*

Go through your steps one by one:

1. What is the verb? was buried.

2. What was buried? The black cat. The black cat is the subject of the sentence.

3. What does the prepositional phrase tell you? *Where* the black cat was buried. *Behind the wall* is a prepositional phrase which acts as an adverb in this sentence, describing or modifying the verb "was buried."

One more time:

> *Before school* is the best time to take a shower.

1. What is the verb? is.

2. When is? "Before school" is. In this sentence, the prepositional phrase is the subject of the sentence. Since the subject of a sentence is always a noun, the prepositional phrase here acts as a noun.

Prepositional phrases *usually* act as adverbs or adjectives. When in doubt, ask yourself what the phrase is telling you in the sentence. When you are picking apart sentences for class or homework, it is usually very helpful to put parentheses around prepositional phrases—they always work together and sometimes they are distracting when you are trying to locate a subject and verb. For example:

> One of the boys in the group of a million is going to join us.

Now, that's a long and complicated sentence. But if you gather together the prepositional phrases like this:

> One (of the boys) (in the group) (of a million) is going to join us.

It may then be clearer for you to see the verb (is going) and the subject (one). If you feel confused, try this. It will probably clear up the structure of a sentence for you.

Prepositional Phrases

Find the prepositional phrase or phrases in each sentence. Put parentheses around them.

1. At the house, Sydney put some ice on her nose.
2. Jake, in the kitchen, asked her if she wanted some soda.
3. The group of them, Amanda, Sydney, and Jake, were pretty shaken up.
4. As always, Amanda felt triumphant in her apartment.
5. Back at the pool, Billy was getting ready for a swim.

Verbal Phrases

Verbal phrases look like verbs: they have verbs in them, but they are not verbs. They will always act as nouns, adjectives, or adverbs. We will talk more about verbal phrases on pages 65-68.

CLAUSES

A clause is a group of words which includes a subject and a verb. There are two types of clauses: dependent and independent. An **independent clause**, which is also called a **principal clause**, makes sense standing alone. A **dependent clause** is used like an adjective, adverb, or noun. It depends on the other clause in the sentence to make sense.

Billy told us that he would come to the party.

This is a sentence that is made up of two separate clauses:

Billy told us   that he would come to the party.

clause 1   *clause 2*

Both of these clauses have subjects and verbs. But the first clause, *Billy told us*, is the independent clause, or principal clause in the sentence, because it could stand alone. *That he would come to the party* is the dependent clause. It wouldn't make sense by itself, and the words work together to modify the verb "told." Billy told us *what*? *That he would come to the party.*

✍ QUIZ #14 ✍
Phrases and Clauses

Each of the following sentences has either a prepositional phrase or a dependent clause with the main, independent clause. Put parentheses around the phrases and underline the dependent clauses.

1. After the party, Alison called Jane.
2. Unless you were there, you wouldn't believe it!
3. Jane called her sister before she found out.
4. Sydney told Jake about the incident.
5. When he returned, Billy spoke to Amanda.

Phrases and Clauses Review

- A **phrase** is a group of words that does not have a subject and a verb.

- The words in a phrase work together as a part of speech.

- **Prepositional phrases** always begin with a preposition and end with a noun.

- A **clause** is a group of words with a subject and a verb.

- A **dependent clause** cannot stand alone as a sentence.

- An **independent clause** makes sense by itself.

Simple, Compound, and Complex Sentences

Some sentences are long and complicated, while others are short and simple. When you first learned to write, you probably wrote all short sentences. But that would be boring after a while. Look at this paragraph:

> We went to the game. We sat in the sun. It was hot. We ate hot dogs. They were delicious.

As compared to: We went to the game. We sat in the sun and it was hot. The hot dogs we ate were delicious.

As you get better at writing, you will want to include some compound and complex sentences. Read on.

Simple Sentences

A simple sentence is made up of one clause. Now, you may have more than one noun in the subject, or more than one word in the predicate, but it can still be simple.

> Apples are my favorite.

> Apple and cherry are my favorite pies.

> Apples make delicious cider or pie.

> I like eating and drinking apple things.

In all of these examples, you cannot separate the sentence into two or more clauses.

Compound Sentences

A compound sentence is made up of two or more independent clauses (or simple sentences) which are joined together with a conjunction. For example:

> We hiked to the picnic grounds *and* we ate our lunches.

> The movie was wonderful *and* I would see it again.

Zippy would eat fruit, *but* he hated vegetables.

Would you like to eat vegetables *or* would you rather have candy?

To decide if a sentence is compound, try to divide it into two or more complete sentences. If you can, then the sentence is compound.

Complex Sentences

A complex sentence has at least one independent clause and at least one dependent clause. You could break the sentence apart, and each part would have a subject and a verb, but at least one of the parts wouldn't make sense alone.

Iggy went to the store *where he bought JuJu fruits*.

He was convinced *that JuJu fruits were as good as real fruit*.

As you can see, some of these clauses could stand alone as sentences, and some of them could not.

You may have noticed that a series of simple sentences can be turned into compound or complex sentences, depending on how you connect them. By the same token, if your compound or complex sentences begin to get *too* compound or complex, it may be easier to break them into smaller, simple sentences. Sometimes you can take a whole long dependent clause and turn it into a simple adjective:

Martha lives in a house <u>which is made of bricks</u>.

Martha lives in a brick house.

Now, both of these sentences are correct, but the second certainly sounds better. Some sentences sound better when they are long and interesting, and some sound better when they are short and simple. Mix them up. Be creative. Reread your sentences to make sure they sound good. Work on developing your "ear" for good grammar and good style.

Compound Sentences

Rewrite each of these simple sentences as one compound sentence.

1. Amanda came home. She found Billy on her couch.

   _____

   _____

2. Billy told her to cool out. He would leave.

   _____

   _____

3. I want to cool out! She won't let me!

   _____

   _____

Now try rewriting these simple sentences as complex ones.

4. She ate pizza. It was her favorite food.

   _____

   _____

5. She ate it every day. It was fattening.

   _____

   _____

6. She ate the pizza. She ate brownies.

   _____

   _____

Now turn the following complicated, confusing sentences into one or two simple sentences.

7. JuJu fruits, which are red, are the most nutritious.

_____

_____

8. If you are going to San Francisco, which can be very foggy, make sure you bring your flashlight.

_____

_____

9. Eating hot dogs can be great, but Maria ate fifteen every day for lunch and soon began to feel sick about the whole thing.

_____

_____

_____

Sentence Review

- A **simple sentence** has one independent clause— a subject and a verb.

- A **compound sentence** has two or more independent clauses joined together with a conjunction. If you take it apart, the two clauses will make sense as separate sentences.

- A **complex sentence** has at least one independent clause and at least one dependent clause.

✍ QUIZ #16 ✍
Putting it all Together

In the following sentences, circle the verbs, underline the subject, and put parentheses around the prepositional phrases. Also, mark "S" if it is a simple sentence, "C" if it is a compound sentence, and "X" if it is a complex sentence.

____ 1. Jennifer asked Sondra what it was that she wanted.

____ 2. I need help!

____ 3. Barnaby and Sondra offered to buy Bridget some fresh bubble gum.

____ 4. Do you still think this ticket, even though we've had some misadventures, is so bad?

____ 5. After she thought about it, Bridget was convinced that her friends were right.

____ 6. Even though we've had some problems, I still think this could be fun.

____ 7. Let's go!

____ 8. We will all be together.

____ 9. We've had some bad luck, but we will try again.

One Last Note . . .

Okay, you've gotten through the first half of the book. In the second half, you're going to hear a lot more terms, and it may feel sort of confusing at first. Just remember the basics, and never hesitate to turn back and review something. All the terms you've learned are also in the glossary in the back, so remember to check there as well.

Chapter 3
The Details and Putting it all Together

In chapters 1 and 2 of this book, we went over each of the basic parts of speech, and the main parts and types of sentences. There's a lot more to know about each of these things, however. As you may know, teachers can ask about strange sounding things like "gerunds" and "infinitives" and "reflexive pronouns." Well, don't let the names of these things put you off. We're going to explain them here too, so you will know what they are.

As you practice grammar and develop your "ear," you will find that you use many of these things naturally in your speech. Speaking and writing properly takes practice. Work on one or two things at a time and master each. Now we are going to review all the things we learned in chapter 1, and talk about each in more detail.

Nouns

Okay, you know that a noun is a person, place, thing, or idea, right? Now, you can change a noun to show different things. For example, you can show that there is more than one noun by making it plural. Or you can show that a noun "owns" something by making it possessive.

Singular and Plural Nouns

If you have one of something, you use a **singular noun** to refer to it. If you have two or more somethings, you use the **plural** form of the noun.

> If you build a second *house*, you have two *houses*.

> If you find a second *mouse*, you don't have two *mouses*!

No, you have two *mice*. You know that your life would be so much easier if you had simple rules to follow. And inconsistencies make people hate grammar. But, there are some pretty consistent rules you can follow to show if you have more than one of something. Yes, there will always be exceptions. We'll try to cover as many of them as possible. But first, let's go over the rules.

- You can make most words plural just by adding an *s* at the end. For example:

alien/aliens	helicopter/helicopters	pizza/pizzas
book/books	joy/joys	soda/sodas
day/days	pickle/pickles	word/words

- If a word ends in *s, x, z, sh*, or *ch*, then you must add *es*.

   Why? Well, just because it sounds better. Those words need a different plural ending, or the plural would just run into the word. For example, we say "box-es" not "boxs." Add the *es* ending when you hear yourself adding a whole new syllable at the end.

box/boxes	Jones/Joneses	tax/taxes
dress/dresses	lunch/lunches	waltz/waltzes
fox/foxes	mess/messes	wish/wishes

- If a word ends in *f* or *fe*, change the ending to a *v* then add *es*.

    Why? Well, it also just sounds better. And, lucky you, it's another rule to remember.

calf/calves	knife/knives	loaf/loaves
elf/elves	leaf/leaves	shelf/shelves
half/halves	life/lives	thief/thieves

- Change *y* to *i* and add *es* if the *y* comes after a consonant. If the *y* comes after a vowel, just add *s*.

| baby/babies | lady/ladies | penny/pennies |
| key/keys | monkey/monkeys | story/stories |

- The weird ones:

    Sometimes there are no rules! Some nouns change completely, and some don't change at all when they go from singular to plural. What do you do? If you are ever unsure about a plural, look it up. In the dictionary, any unusual plurals are listed right after the singular form of the word. Here we go:

child/children	moose/moose	sheep/sheep
deer/deer	mouse/mice	tooth/teeth
foot/feet	person/people	woman/women

✍ QUIZ #17 ◿
Singular and Plural Nouns

Change the singular nouns in parentheses to plural nouns.

1. Sondra asked Jennifer to eat fifteen (banana) _____.

2. Taylor told me that his twelve (monkey) _____ escaped from their (cage) _____ and wanted to wash their (foot) _____ in the bath.

3. My favorite (movie) _____ are (comedy) _____.

4. If you are going to put (fox) _____ in (box) _____, you'd better not bring them to (church) _____ or feed them (lunch) _____.

5. The shoemaker's (elf) _____ put the (shoe) _____ on the (shelf) _____ all by themselves.

6. One of the great (joy) _____ of eating (burger) _____ is that you don't need (knife) _____.

7. "Do you know where the (lady) _____ who sold me these (shoe) _____ are?" asked Babette.

8. "I believe they are hiding in the (bush) _____ or behind that group of (man) _____," Taylor replied.

9. If you clear the (dish) _____ from the table, make sure you wrap the (leftover) _____ and put the (bowl) _____ in the refrigerator.

10. If you take out the (paint) _____, wash the (paintbrush) _____ before you use them.

Collective Nouns

A **collective noun** is a group noun. Because it refers to a group of people who usually act together as a group, the noun is almost always treated as singular. If the members of the group do not act together, the noun is plural. Some examples of collective nouns are: *audience, jury, government, furniture.*

Look at the following sentences:

> The jury was selected by the lawyers.
> (The noun is singular because it refers to one group, chosen together.)

> The jury were in disagreement about the verdict.
> (The noun is plural because it refers to people acting in disagreement.)

Possessive Nouns

If a person, place, or thing "owns" something, you can use a **possessive noun**. It will make your sentences sound much more smooth and clear. For example, instead of:

> the coat *of Bert*

> the sweater *of Ernie*

> a vacation *of a week*

Say:

> *Bert's* coat

> *Ernie's* sweater

> a *week's* vacation

Whenever you can substitute a phrase that begins with "of" and ends with a noun, you use the possessive form of the noun instead.

Now, as you know, a noun is either singular or plural. That will affect how you make it into a possessive.

• If a noun is singular, always add 's, even if it ends in s. For example:

Bert	Bert's hat
Charles	Charles's homework
dress	dress's hemline
girl	girl's house
James	James's bicycle

Okay, we admit that *James's* looks a little odd. And, to be honest, if you wrote *James'* that would be okay as well. But, to be safe and to keep your rules as simple as possible, remember that all singular nouns get –'s when made possessive.

• If a noun is plural but it doesn't end in *s*, add –'s. If it does end in *s*, add –'. Here we go:

babies	babies' room
children	children's room
ladies	ladies' room
men	men's room

To summarize, just add –'s to any noun to show it is possessive, unless it is a plural noun ending in *s*.

✍ QUIZ #18 ✍
Possessives

Fill in the missing parts of the following chart.

Singular	Singular possessive	Plural	Plural possessive
berry cat desk dog family glove house Jones peach thief			

Direct and Indirect Objects

Remember that to find the subject of a sentence, first ask yourself what the verb is, and then what is doing that action. That's the subject. The **direct object** of the sentence is the receiver of the action. Let's start with a simple sentence:

Bozo threw confetti.

What's the verb? Threw. Who threw? Bozo. Bozo is the subject of the sentence. He does the throwing. What is getting thrown? Confetti. So, confetti is the direct object of the sentence.

Now, you must have a direct object before you have an **indirect object**. If we give you more information about this event (Bozo threw the audience confetti), the audience is the indirect object. It tells you "to whom" or "for whom" the action was being done. You can always spot an indirect object by pulling it out and making a prepositional phrase with it. In this case, you might have said:

Bozo threw confetti (at the audience).

One more time:

Zelda gave Zorba a fancy jacket.

Zelda is the subject. What is the direct object and what is the indirect object of the verb gave? What did she give? A fancy jacket. That is the direct object. Zorba is the indirect object and you can check by making it into a prepositional phrase:

Zelda gave a fancy jacket (to Zorba).

It is also worth remembering that if you have both a direct object and an indirect object, the indirect object usually comes between the verb and the direct object.

Finding Direct and Indirect Objects

In each of the following sentences, circle the direct object and underline the indirect object (if one exists).

1. Dylan told Brenda the bad news.
2. Brenda sold Tiffani rights to the story.
3. The police asked Dylan several questions.
4. We wanted bananas and peeled grapes for the party.
5. Brandon ate ninety-eight bananas before winning the contest.

Predicate Nouns

One kind of noun you find in the predicate of a sentence is an object (direct or indirect.) But some verbs do not take objects. The most common example is the verb *to be* (is, are, will, am, etc.). The verb *to be* is like an equals sign. In this case, the noun in the predicate will rename or explain the subject. Other verbs, that may take predicate nouns instead of direct objects, are *to become, to seem, to appear.* You can always tell a predicate noun or pronoun because it will be equal to the subject.

> *Krusty is my favorite clown.*
> (Krusty = clown, so clown is the predicate noun.)

> *Homer is a strange father.*
> (Homer = father, so father is the predicate noun.)

> *Springfield is the largest city in the state.*
> (Springfield = city, so city is the predicate noun.)

Not all sentences have predicate nouns. To tell if a noun is a predicate noun or a direct object just ask yourself if it equals the subject.

> *Lisa plays the saxophone.*
> (Lisa = saxophone? No, so, saxophone is the direct object.)

Lisa is the lead in the play.

(Lisa = lead? Yes, so *lead* is the predicate noun.)

✍ QUIZ #20 ✍
Identifying Predicate Nouns

Underline the predicate nouns in the following sentences.

1. Bart is an intrepid explorer.
2. Always afraid of his shadow, Mr. Burns is a coward.
3. That kid with the glasses is Milhouse.
4. Maggie is the youngest child.
5. Homer seems like a new man.

PRONOUNS

Remember that a pronoun takes the place of a noun.

Personal Pronouns

Personal pronouns take on different forms depending on to whom they refer.

First person refers to the speaker: *I, me, mine, my, we, us, our, ours* are all the pronouns you would use if you were speaking in the first person (the speaker is talking about herself).

Second person refers to the person being spoken to: *you, your, yours* are second person pronouns. Use them when you are speaking directly to someone.

Third person refers to the person being spoken about: *he, him, his, she, her, hers, it, its, they, them, their, theirs* are used when you are talking about another person.

Formal reports

Most teachers prefer you not to use the second person, "you," in your written work, because it is the most informal of the personal pronouns. It is usually preferable to use the pronoun "one." Check with your teacher if you are not sure. Here is an example. You can say:

> One will see the insect species I have described in the picture below.

Or:

> The insect species I have described is shown in the picture below.

But not:

> You will see the insect species I have described in the picture below.

Pronoun Case

There are two sets of personal pronouns—subject pronouns and object pronouns. *Subject* pronouns are referred to as the **nominative case**. *Object* pronouns are referred to as the **objective case**.

Nominative (subject) pronouns

Singular	Plural
I	we
you	you
he	they
she	they
it	

Use subject pronouns:

- As the subject of a verb. The subject of the verb is the doer of the action.

> *She* threw the ball. (Who threw? *She.*)
>
> *I* went to the party. (Who went? *I.*)
>
> *We* wanted ice cream. (Who wanted? *We.*)
>
> *They* came to our store. (Who came? *They.*)

- After using a form of the verb *to be* (am, is, are, or will, for example). Remember, the verb *to be* is like an equals sign; anything after it will be the same form as before. If you have a subject noun before, you need a subject pronoun after. You can think of this as the "phone rule." It's the way you answer the phone—when someone calls and says "I'm looking for a Ms. Oakley," you answer, "This is she."

Objective (object) pronouns

Singular	Plural
me	us
you	you
her	them
him	them
it	

Use object pronouns:

- As the direct object of a verb. The subject of a verb is the doer of the action. The direct object of the verb is the receiver of the action.

    She asked *me* to come to the party. (Who did she ask? *Me.*)

    I picked *them*. (I picked what? *Them.*)

- As the indirect object of a verb. An indirect object is not the receiver of the action.

    I picked *her* flowers.

    Marlyn gave *him* a punch in the nose.

- As the object of a preposition.

    I gave the flowers to *her*.

    We ran with *them* to the race.

Some tips

One of the most common errors people make is to confuse the subject and object pronouns. There are a few common pitfalls you can avoid with practice.

- Say, "between you and me . . ."

  It's not between you and I. The pronouns are the objects of the preposition *between* and are always in object form. So it would be "between you and him," or "between me and him," or whatever pronouns you use.

- If you are making a comparison, complete the comparison in your head to decide if you need a subject or object pronoun.

  > Sally is smarter than *I/me*.

  Finish the comparison: Sally is smarter than *I* am.

  > She is as tall as *he/him*.

  Finish the comparison: She is as tall as *he* is.

  This one sounds a little strange, so you have to practice it.

- If you have a compound subject or predicate, try saying each one separately to figure it out.

  > Bob and *I/me* went to the store.

  To check:

  > Bob went to the store.

  > *I* went to the store.

  > Mary went with Paul and *him/he*.

  To check:

  > Mary went with Paul.

  > Mary went with *him*.

• What about . . .

We/Us kids went on the hike last Saturday

To check:

Take out the kids: *We* went on the hike last Saturday, so *we* is correct.

✍ QUIZ #21 ✍
Babette Goes to Beverly Hills, Again

Underline the correct pronoun in each of the following sentences.

After returning from Beverly Hills, Barnaby looked at Babette. (He, Him) wanted to know what (she, her) thought of that trip.

"Darling, that is not the real Beverly Hills, believe (I, me). The real Beverly Hills is the place where you meet Brenda, Tiffani, Brandon, and Dylan. Let (us, we) go there," Babette cried.

"Do you think (us, we) really should try again?" Bridget wondered.

"(Us, we) will never know the truth unless (us, we) try again!" Babette told (they, them).

"Between you and (I, me)," Jennifer whispered to Bridget, "(I, me) don't care if (I, me) ever see Beverly Hills again."

"Give (I, me) the ticket, darling." Babette rubbed. "Oh, Dylan, (I, me) can't wait to meet you."

The clubhouse rumbled. Thwump! (They, Them) landed in Dylan's yard.

"Who's there?" (they, them) heard a voice call from the kitchen.

Possessive Pronouns

Now, you know that you need to add -'s to make a noun possessive. But with pronouns, it's a different story. The possessive pronouns do *not* take an apostrophe at all. Take a look at the personal pronouns and their possessive forms.

Personal pronoun	Possessive form
I, me	my
you	your
he, him	his
she, her	hers
we, us	ours
they, them	theirs
it	its
who, whom	whose

So, there is no apostrophe in the possessive form of these pronouns. You don't want to confuse the possessive form with the contraction:

its (possessive form)   *it's* (contraction standing for *it is*)

whose (possessive form)   *who's* (contraction standing for *who is*)

Relative, Reflexive, Demonstrative, and Interrogative Pronouns

Okay, don't panic. These are actually pretty easy. Let's look at them one at a time.

Relative pronouns

These pronouns link a relative clause to the main clause of a sentence. There are two types of relative pronouns, definite and indefinite. **Definite relative pronouns** stand for a definite noun. **Indefinite relative pronouns** are not preceded by a definite noun (also called an antecedent).

Definite relative pronouns	Indefinite relative pronouns
which	what
that	which
who	who
whom	whatever
	whom
	whomever

> Zelda went to see F. Scott, *who* was quite dashing in his white suit.

The main clause of this sentence is *Zelda went to see F. Scott*. *Who was quite dashing in his white suit* is a relative clause because it cannot stand alone. Here it modifies, or describes, F. Scott. The relative pronoun, *who*, links the two clauses.

The following are the rules for relative pronouns:

- If you are deciding between **who** and **whom**, just substitute he and him. If you would use he, then use who. If you would use him, then use whom.

- **Who** and **whom** refer to people.

- **That** can refer to people, animals, or things.

- **Which** cannot refer to people.

- **That** and **which** are commonly misused and confused. In general, if you are referring to a part of the group in your clause, use *that*. If you are talking about the whole group, use *which*. *Which* generally follows a comma; *that* doesn't.

> I like apples *that* are green and tart. (I'm only talking about a part of the group of apples—those that are green and tart, so use *that*.)

> I like apples, *which* are very healthy and good to eat. (I'm talking about all apples, so use *which*.)

Relative Pronoun Time

Underline the correct relative pronoun in each of the following sentences.

1. Sideshow Bob, (who, whom) is Krusty's faithful sidekick, was after Bart.

2. *The Krusty the Clown Show*, (which, that) is Lisa's favorite, is on at 4 p.m. each day.

3. The Itchy and Scratchy episode, (which, that) Bart and Lisa like the best, is quite gory.

4. Could these be the children (who, whom) I brought into the world?

5. Maggie's favorite pacifier is the one (that, which) makes the most noise.

Reflexive pronouns

When you think of reflexive pronouns, think about reflections—they are just like mirrors. They refer to the subject in the sentence. The reflexive pronouns are *myself, yourself, herself, himself, ourselves, yourselves, themselves, itself.* Read through the following rules:

• Make sure that the reflexive pronoun agrees with the noun it mirrors.

> I, *myself*, really like pizza.

> They went around talking about *themselves*.

> David, *himself*, ate all fifty cookies.

• You may use them for emphasis, but don't go crazy.

> He, *himself*, won the championship.

> I, *myself*, am quite proud of my accomplishment.

• Don't substitute reflexive pronouns for subject pronouns.

> Paul and *I* went to the museum.

Not:

> Paul and *myself* went to the museum.

Demonstrative pronouns

A demonstrative pronoun demonstrates which noun in the sentence is being talked about. The demonstrative pronouns are *that, these, this,* and *those.* Here are the rules:

- A demonstrative pronoun must take the place of a specific noun. Otherwise, it is really just an adjective:

  > I want to drink all of **this**. (*This* refers to something the speaker is pointing to, such as Coke or milk or apple juice, so it is a demonstrative pronoun.)

  > **This** dress is new. (*This* is an adjective, describing a dress. Which dress? This dress.)

  > **Those** are completely worthless! (*Those* refers to something the speaker is pointing to, so it is a demonstrative pronoun.)

  > **Those** books are completely worthless! (*Those* is an adjective, modifying books. Which books? Those books.)

- Remember, demonstrative pronouns are not an excuse for being imprecise. You need to let your reader or listener know what it is you are referring to.

Interrogative pronouns

As the name suggests, these pronouns are used to ask questions. The interrogative, or question pronouns, are *who, whom, which,* and *what.*

> **Who** are you?

> **What** do you want?

> **Which** house do you live in?

> **Whom** do you want to see?

Pronoun Agreement

While this is the last pronoun thing we are covering, it is one of the most important. You must be sure when you use a pronoun that it agrees in number with the noun it replaces: Use a *singular* pronoun to replace a *singular* noun. Use a *plural* pronoun to replace a *plural* noun. For example:

> Gilligan found *two coconuts* and ate *them* up.

> *Mary Ann* put *her* new bathing suit on.

As with all rules, there are a couple of points to keep in mind.

The A NOSE rule

As a rule, use singular pronouns to refer back to any of these words: anybody, anything, nobody, nothing, neither, one, someone, something, each, every, and either. You can remember them because they begin with the letters A, N, O, S, or E. For example:

> The professor felt that *everyone* should do *his* part on the island.

> *Neither* Mary Ann nor Ginger felt *she* was going to be rescued.

Now, as you can see, this rule may sometimes lead to awkward sounding sentences. You might end up saying things like:

> When *a boy or a girl* tries out for sports, *he* should practice.

Technically, that's correct. But realistically it sounds stupid, and sexist. What happened to the girl? Should you say:

> When a boy or a girl tries out for sports, *he or she* should practice.

Yikes! You're being even more awkward with that one. How about:

> When a boy or a girl tries out for sports, *they* should practice.

We'll be honest—this is how most people handle it. But it's wrong! Sloppy! Don't fall for the "they" trap. They has become an all-purpose pronoun used by people who can't dig themselves out of the grammar trap. What to do? When in doubt: *rewrite*. How about:

> When *boys and girls* try out for sports, *they* should practice.

By rewriting the whole sentence with a plural subject, you get to use the nice easy plural pronoun "they." You haven't offended anyone and your sentence is grammatically correct. Be consistent.

• Remember not to switch pronouns in a sentence.

> *You* must turn on *your* stereo before listening to *your* music.

Not:

> *One* must turn on *your* stereo before listening to *one's* music.

• Make the nouns that go with your pronouns consistent in number.

> *Each* of the boys asked for *a raise* in *his* allowance.

Not:

> *Each* of the boys asked for *raises* in *his* allowance.
> (Remember: one boy, one raise.)

> *All* the students took *books* out of the library.

Not:

> *All* the students took *a book* out of the library.
> (Remember: more than one student, more than one book. Unless, of course, they were all taking out the same book.)

- Make sure your reader knows which noun you are referring to when you use a pronoun. Look at the following sentence.

> Mr. Howell and the Skipper were sure that *he* could get them off the island.

He, who? Were they sure that Mr. Howell, with all his money, could get them off the island? Or were they sure that the Skipper, with his sailing expertise, could get them off the island? You would have to say the following if that's what you meant:

> Mr. Howell and the Skipper were sure that *the Skipper* could get them off the island.

✍ QUIZ #23 ✍
Pronoun Agreement

Cross out the incorrect pronoun in each sentence and replace it with a better one.

1. Either Ginger or Mary Ann was sure to have brought their new bathing suit.

2. Anybody who has seen *Gilligan's Island* is certain to know that they have seen a classic.

3. "If anyone finds a way off this island, would they please let us know?" cried Mr. Howell.

4. "Oh, lovey," called Mrs. Howell, "neither Gilligan nor you is able to figure out what they really want."

5. "All of them are happy as clams to be here. We want to stay on this island forever!" cried Mary Ann.

VERBS

Verbs are the very heart of a sentence. They express action or states of being. Without a verb, you cannot have a sentence. So, you might say that verbs are the most important part of a sentence. There's a lot to do here, so let's get started.

Subject-Verb Agreement

You must make sure that the subject and verb agree in number: *Singular* subjects take *singular* verbs. *Plural* subjects take *plural* verbs.

How simple could life be? How do you recognize a singular and a plural verb? Well, in general, you add *s* to a noun to make it *plural,* and add *s* to a verb to make it *singular.* Strange, but true. Check it out:

Singular	**Plural**
The girl jumps.	The girls jump.
The kitten frolics.	The kittens frolic.
The fat lady sings.	The fat ladies sing.
The shark swims.	The sharks swim.

Of course, this isn't true for all verbs, but it is true for many. In general, you must first check the subject, then ask yourself if the subject is singular or plural, then make sure the verbs match.

> *Greg and Cindy were* afraid of the ghost that haunted the attic.

> *My sister,* the silly one, *was* sick of figs.

Don't be fooled by a group of words that may separate the subject and the verb. Remember to bracket off the prepositional phrases—they are never part of the subject.

> The *bunch* (of kids) (in the yard) *is* going to sing a song.

> *One* (of the several thousand) (in the state) *was* going to make it to the semi-finals.

Subject-Verb tips

- Bracket off prepositional phrases—they are never part of the subject.

- Locate the verb. Ask yourself who or what is doing the action.

- Locate the subject.

- Do the subject and the verb match? Plural subjects take plural verbs, singular subjects take singular verbs.

- Subjects joined by *and* are plural. Subjects joined by *or* are singular.

> Jan *or* Cindy *is* going to win.

> Greg *and* Bobby *are* the best around.

✍ QUIZ #24 ✍
Subject-Verb Agreement

Match the correct verb with the subject in the following sentences.

1. Alice (*cook, cooks*) for the kids every night.

2. Every night, she (*make, makes*) their favorite meal: meatloaf.

3. "(*Wasn't, weren't*) we going to have something different tonight, Alice?" (*ask, asks*) Cindy.

4. "Yikes! Meatloaf again!" (*cries, cry*) Jan and Marcia. "We need to watch our figures!"

5. "(*Doesn't, don't*) you people have anything better to do than worry about dinner?" (*wonder, wonders*) Alice.

6. "Oh, no, not meatloaf!" (*yell, yells*) Mr. or Mrs. Brady from upstairs.

7. "Oh, I (*am, is*) sick of trying to please all of you finicky Bradys!" Alice says as she (*stomp, stomps*) out of the house for the last time.

Tenses

Verbs not only tell you what happened, they tell you *when* it happened. The "when" part is called the verb **tense**. There are three main tenses: past, present, and future.

Past tense

This is the tense you use whenever you are talking or writing about something that has already happened:

> Yesterday, I *fell* down.

> An hour ago, I *went* to the store.

> Once upon a time, a beautiful princess *was born*.

Anytime the action takes place in the past, whether it was an hour or a thousand years ago, you use the past tense. Most stories are written in the past tense—it is the easiest and most natural way to tell a story.

✍ QUIZ #25 ✍
Mr. Brady! Save us from Dylan!

Change all the present tense verbs that don't make sense to the past tense.

Dylan comes into the yard and sees the clubhouse. The kids are shaking when they hear him yell and scream. "This clubhouse! Why is it landing in my yard?"

Babette looks out of the window. "What a hunk!" she cries. "But he is being so violent. I am scared."

"Get out of here, or I'll call the police."

"Quick, give me the ticket. I have an idea," Taylor says. He rubs the ticket and cries, "Help us, Mr. Brady!"

Suddenly, Mr. Brady walks into the yard. "Hey!" he yells, "stop hitting that clubhouse!"

Dylan turns around. "This is my yard, man. I'll hit what I want."

"Excuse me, kids, but who lives here?"

"He does," Babette points sheepishly toward Dylan.

"Sorry, bud. My mistake." Mr. Brady picks up a stick and waves it at the house with Dylan. "Okay, you kids, get out of here or I'll have to call the police."

"*Anna banana!*" Taylor throws his hands up in disgust.

Present tense

This is the tense you use to show that something is happening right now.

> I *am* here.

> Right now, I *am listening* to my best friend.

It can also be used to show something you do all the time:

> Every day at three, I *run* to the track for practice.

> I *take* a shower every morning.

You should use the present tense when you are stating something you know for a fact:

> Green Day *is* the best band around.

Future tense

This is the tense that is used to show what is going to happen.

> Tomorrow, I *will go* to the Green Day show.

> In an hour, I *will run* in the race.

> Next year, I *will be* in high school.

Now, there are more than three tenses; in fact, there are twelve altogether. Before we talk about how the different tenses are formed, we have to talk about the principal parts of the verb.

Principal parts

Three forms of a verb are the most important—they are used to form the different tenses. They are called the principal parts of the verb, and they are the **present tense**, the **past tense** and the **past participle**.

Regular verbs

A regular verb is a verb in which the principal parts are all formed the same way—the past tense and past participle are formed by adding *ed, d,* or *t* to the present tense. For example:

Present	Past	Past participle
ask	asked	asked
climb	climbed	climbed
dive	dived	dived
drag	dragged	dragged
drown	drowned	drowned
sneak	sneaked	sneaked

The perfect tenses

Use the **present perfect** if:

- The action started in the past and continues to the present.

  I *have sneaked* two miles so far. (I am still *sneaking.*)

- The action started in the past and was finished at an earlier time.

  I *have sneaked* 150 miles in my spy-training routine so far.

Use the **past perfect** if:

- You want to show one thing that happened in the past, before something else that happened in the past.

> Before I sneaked to his house, I *had sneaked* to three other houses.

Use the **future perfect** if:

- You want to show an action that will be completed at some future time (this is a rarely used tense).

> By next Tuesday, I *will have sneaked* around the whole neighborhood.

Tenses tip

Four of the tenses have words that tip you off to them:

Future: *shall* or *will*

Present perfect: *has* or *have*

Past perfect: *had*

Future perfect: *shall have,* or *will have*

Helping Verbs

You may have noticed that many sentences have verbs that are more than one word long. Verbs may be two or three words long, as you can see in the future perfect tense. For example, in this case, there is a main verb and one or two helping verbs:

> He *will have eaten* all my favorite cookies by next week.

> Here, *will have* are the helping verbs to the main verb, *eaten*.

Tenses

Fill in the correct verb form in each blank. The verb is in the infinitive form at the end of each sentence.

1. Yesterday, Barnaby _____ twenty-seven chocolate chip cookies. (to eat)

2. Before he finished the cookies, he _____ four dozen. (to bake)

3. Right now, Bridget _____ her favorite bubble gum. (to chew)

4. Tomorrow, Barnaby and Bridget _____ to Jennifer's house. (to go)

5. By next Wednesday, Barnaby _____ another thirty batches of chocolate chip cookies. (to bake)

Irregular Verbs

Irregular verbs are verbs that do not follow the standard formula for making the past tense and past participles. Some irregular verbs are so common that you don't really have to think about them. *To be* is an irregular verb—but you know it so well because you use it all the time: I am, I was, I have been, I will have been.

Principal parts of some irregular verbs

Present	Past	Past participle
bear	bore	borne
blow	blew	blown
bring	brought (not brang)	brought
creep	crept	crept
draw	drew	drawn
drink	drank	drunk
freeze	froze	frozen
get	got	got, gotten
grow	grew	grown

hang	hung	hung (as in I hung a picture)
	hanged	hanged (as in the man was hanged)
lay	laid	laid (I laid the book down)
lie	lay	lain (I have lain in bed)
ring	rang	rung
shake	shook	shaken
shrink	shrank, shrunk	shrunk, shrunken
sink	sank	sunk
slay	slew	slain
spring	sprang, sprung	sprung
swear	swore	sworn
swim	swam	swum
tear	tore	torn
weep	wept	wept
wring	wrung	wrung

✍ QUIZ #27 ✍
Correct Verb Forms

Underline the correct form of the verb in each sentence.

1. Max (wept, weeped) when he heard the bad news.
2. "My brother has been (hung, hanged)!" he cried.
3. "I have (laid, lain) on my bed too long!" he swore.
4. "If I had (slew, slain) that criminal, my poor brother would still be alive."
5. "I (brang, brought) this on myself," thought Max.

What Is Voice?

You may use two types of voices when you are writing—the active voice and the passive voice. The **active voice** is when the subject is performing the action. The **passive voice** is when the action happens to the subject. For example:

Active: Michael drove the car.

Passive: The car was driven by Michael.

As you can imagine, it is preferable to use the active voice when you are writing. It is almost always the more direct, clearer way to say something. When you use the passive voice, you usually write a muddled, confused sentence.

One more time:

Active: We went to the movies.

Passive: The movies were gone to by us.

Active: Cats purr to indicate contentment.

Passive: Purring indicates contentment by cats.

Verbals

A verbal is one of three types of phrases—participles, gerunds, and infinitives—that looks like a verb, but acts like a noun, adjective, or adverb.

Participles

It looks like a verb, but it isn't. You can think of a participle as a verb that acts like an adjective in a sentence. It looks just like a verb but it isn't complete. Look at the difference:

> I *had fallen* down the stairs.

> The leaf, *fallen* from the tree, was quite beautiful.

In the first sentence, *had fallen* is the verb. In the second, the past participle *fallen* is used by itself as an adjective to describe the leaf.

One more time:

> I *had known* that he would be famous one day.

> *Known* for his great laugh, Billy was famous.

In the first sentence, *had known* is the main verb in the sentence. *Known* in the second sentence describes Billy; it is an adjective.

✍ QUIZ #28 ✍
Find the Participles

Put brackets around the participle phrases in the following sentences.

1. Discovering his missing buffalo ribs, Fred called for Wilma.
2. Using the information gathered in his research, Barney quickly figured out who the culprit was.
3. "This dish, placed here by Wilma, has been tampered with!" cried Betty.
4. Bam Bam, wishing to go out, yelled "Bam! Bam!"
5. Pebbles, burping with some guilt, admitted to them all that she had eaten the ribs.

Gerunds

While participles are verbals that are used as adjectives, gerunds are verbals that are used as nouns. Gerunds are easy to spot: they are verbs ending in *-ing*. Check it out:

> *Skating* is my favorite thing to do.

> *Skating* is a noun, and here it acts as the subject of the sentence.

One more time:

> *Collecting* stamps is Edwina's favorite hobby.

> *Collecting* is not a verb in this sentence; it is a noun. *Collecting* is the subject of the verb *is*.

✍ QUIZ #29 ✍
Spotting Gerunds

Underline the gerunds in each of the following sentences.

1. I always liked playing baseball.
2. We all enjoyed running out onto the field.
3. Batting is the one thing I don't do well.
4. Fielding is my area of expertise.
5. Winning, however, is something everybody likes.

Infinitives

Infinitives can be nouns, adjectives, or adverbs. An infinitive is a verb form with the preposition *to*. If you see *to* with a noun, it's a prepositional phrase, but if you see *to* with a verb, it's an infinitive. The infinitives of the verb *help*, for example, are to help, to have helped, to be helped, and to have been helped.

Noun: A doctor hopes *to help* his patients.

Adjective: Which of these books would be the one *to help* me study? (*To help* modifies the noun *the one*.)

Adverb: My sister told us stories *to help* pass the time. (*To help* modifies the verb *told*.)

✍ QUIZ #30 ✍
Infinitives

Spot the infinitive in each of the following sentences. For bonus points, say what part of speech it is.

1. Jethro wanted to see the sights in Beverly Hills.

   _____

2. To go to the races was Granny's favorite pastime.

   _____

3. Mr. Drysdale wanted to eat with the Clampetts.

   _____

4. Elly Mae hoped to win the beauty contest that week.

   _____

MODIFIERS AND PREPOSITIONS
What are the Comparative Forms?

Using the right adjective is easy if you know the rules. Most adjectives have three forms: the positive, the comparative, and the superlative. Use the *positive form* when you are talking about one thing, the *comparative form* when you are comparing two things, and the *superlative form* when you are comparing three or more things.

Positive: Susie is *smart*.

Comparative: Paul is *smarter*.

           (Comparing two things.)

Superlative: Johanna is the *smartest*.

           (Comparing three things.)

The Comparative and the Superlative

If an adjective has only *one* syllable, add *er* for the comparative form, and *est* for the superlative form. If the last letter is *y*, change the *y* to an *i*.

Positive	Comparative	Superlative
slow	slower	slowest
fast	faster	fastest
dry	drier	driest

When an adjective has *two* syllables things get a little trickier. Sometimes you will add *er* for the comparative form and *est* for the superlative form. Sometimes you will add *more* for the comparative form and *most* for the superlative form.

If you are not sure, check the dictionary. It will suggest which comparative and superlative forms to use.

Positive	Comparative	Superlative
silly	sillier	silliest
funny	funnier	funniest
graceful	more graceful	most graceful

If an adjective has three or more syllables, add *more* for the comparative form and *most* for the superlative form.

Positive	Comparative	Superlative
ridiculous	more ridiculous	most ridiculous
argumentative	more argumentative	most argumentative

Some adjectives have irregular comparative and superlative forms. Check out the following examples.

Positive	Comparative	Superlative
bad	worse	worst
good	better	best
little	less	least
many	more	most

For example:

Positive: Jane is friendly.

Comparative: Peter is *less* friendly.

Superlative: Nancy is the *least* friendly.

Some adjectives never take a comparative or superlative form because they express something that is perfect or complete. In other words they cannot be more or less. For example:

unique

perfect

infinite

dead

Something cannot be more unique or less perfect. If you really need to modify these adjectives, you should use adverbs such as almost, more, nearly, or hardly, to show that something approaches these qualities.

nearly perfect

almost dead

hardly unique

Finally, you should always avoid using double comparisons, such as *more uglier, most friendliest.* Say either uglier or friendliest.

✍ QUIZ #31 ✍
Adjectives

Underline the correct adjective form in the following sentences.

1. Of all the kids, Barnaby was the (smarter, smartest).
2. Taylor was (quieter, quietest) than Jennifer.
3. Instead of yummy mashed potatoes or healthy string beans, Bridget likes bubble gum (better, best).
4. Between Sondra and Taylor, Sondra is the (odder, oddest).
5. Babette is the (more, most) mysterious person you have ever met.

Using the Correct Adverb/Adjective

Adverbs and adjectives are commonly confused, because they often sound very similar. If you are unsure if a word is an adverb or an adjective, look it up. Keep in mind that many adverbs end in *-ly*. But, most importantly, remember that adverbs modify verbs, adjectives, and other adverbs, whereas adjectives modify nouns. Look at the following sentences:

> Mary went *quick/quickly* up the stairs. (Use *quickly*, the adverb, because you are describing the verb, went.)

She sure is a *quick/quickly* runner. (Use *quick* because you are describing the noun, runner.)

The good/well confusion

These are words that everybody mixes up. How often have you heard, "I just know you'll do good on that test"? That's wrong. Remember *good* is an adjective and *well* is an adverb. If you are talking about how you will "do," then you need to modify it with an adverb.

That song is *good*. You play it *well*.

This meatloaf is *good*. You cook so *well*.

Well can also be an adjective. When it means "in good health" or "attractive." So, it is correct to say:

You look *well*.

I feel *well*.

✍ QUIZ #32 ✍
Adjectives and Adverbs

Underline the correct word in each of the following sentences.

1. Amanda felt (good, well) on that (beautiful, beautifully) day.

2. Jake wanted (bad, badly) to call her and tell her how (sad, sadly) he felt.

3. Sydney told her sister that she dressed (good, well) for such a (good, well) day.

4. After coming to a (sudden, suddenly) stop, Jake's (new, newly) sports car screeched (loud, loudly).

5. Stomping (forceful, forcefully) out of the room, Amanda flipped her (thick, thickly) blonde hair back from her (cool, coolly) eyes.

Misplaced Modifiers

> Driving down the lonely road, my mind
> wandered and I veered off into a ditch.

Do you know what's wrong with this sentence? It may sound just fine, but look closely at the opening phrase, "Driving down the lonely road." What's driving down the lonely road? Well, it sounds like "my mind" was driving, because that's the closest thing to the modifying phrase.

- The rule for modifiers is simple: Place the modifier as close as possible to the thing it modifies.

Why? Well, to be clear and precise. If you move modifiers all around your sentences with careless abandon, you will confuse your reader. Check it out:

> While eating chocolate chip cookies, the front
> door blew open.

Now, who was eating chocolate chip cookies? The front door? The front door is the subject of the sentence. If you want to be clear that *you* were eating the chocolate chip cookies, and not some scary front door, change the sentence around.

> While I was eating chocolate chip cookies, the
> front door blew open.

Or:

> While eating chocolate chip cookies, I saw the
> front door blow open.

One more time:

> After finishing the race, my shoes stank.

> Again, what finished the race? My shoes? That
> doesn't make sense.

> After I finished the race, my shoes stank.

How could you change the following sentence?

> To make a model rocket, hard work and precision is required.

Try this:

> To make a model rocket, you must work hard and use precision.

What about single word adjectives and adverbs? Look at these two sentences:

> He only voted for David for class president. (meaning he didn't help with the campaign)

> He voted only for David for class president. (meaning he didn't vote for anyone else)

How about?

> Do you ever remember seeing such a wonderful Green Day concert?

Or:

> Do you remember ever seeing such a wonderful Green Day concert?

Well, if you're modifying the verb *seeing*, put the adverb *ever* before and as close to it as possible. The second sentence probably comes closer to the writer's intended meaning.

✍ QUIZ #33 ✍
Misplaced Modifiers

Underline the misplaced modifier, then rewrite each of the following sentences.

1. Approaching his favorite TV star, the professor was right next to Barnaby.

   _____

   _____

2. Hearing the voice of Wilma, the set was filled with excitement for Sondra.

_____

_____

3. Going to the set of the TV show *Beverly Hills 90210*, the ride was bumpy for Babette.

_____

_____

4. Thinking about Amanda, the pole hit a dreamy Jennifer smack in the face.

_____

_____

Using the Correct Preposition

It is not always easy to pick the correct preposition. Some people have a good ear for this sort of thing, but for others that's not the case. While there are few rules concerning the correct use of prepositions, unfortunately there are hundreds of idioms that use prepositions. An idiom is just a way of putting words together. Here are some examples of the more easily confused prepositions.

at, by

Use *by* only when you mean "past" or "by way of."

> He stopped *at* the store after school.

> We went *by* the McDonald's on our way to Burger King.

at, to

Use *to* for motion. When you go to a place, you are *at* it.

> Margot and I were *at* the mall all afternoon.

> We are going *to* the movies later.

at, with

Use *at* for a thing, and *with* for a person.

> I was furious *with* my mother for not letting me go.

> I was angry *at* the new rule at school that doesn't allow us to leave campus.

between, among

Use *between* when you have two things, and *among* for more than two things.

> *Between* you and me, this is the worst party I have been to this year.

> *Among* the fifteen parties I have gone to, this is by far the worst.

> *Between* the English department and the Social Studies department, there are very few good teachers.

(Note: even though there are more than two people in the English department and the Social Studies department, you are talking about two groups, so you use *between*.)

beside, besides

Beside means "next to." *Besides* means "in addition to."

> I want to sit *beside* Jimmy tonight.

> I hope you'll talk to someone *besides* him.

from, off

Don't use *off* when you mean *from*. *"Off of"* is never correct.

> I bought the Green Day CD *from* my favorite store.

> Get *off* the bus at Fourth Street to get to my house.

over, to

You cannot go *over* someone's house unless you have wings. Use *to*.

> We went *to* Marcel's new beach house last summer.

> Batgirl flew *over* our heads.

Idiomatic prepositional phrases which will impress your friends

Do you need to memorize these? Nah. Just read through them to see if there are any you get wrong all the time. Try to work on them. You may also use this list as a reference tool when you are writing.

angry *about* (an idea, a thing): Babette was *angry about* the ridiculous situation they were in.

angry *with* (a person): Babette was *angry with* Simone for causing it.

compare *to* (shows similarity): *Compared to* the *Mona Lisa*, this is really rather good.

compare *with* (shows similarity and difference): You can't *compare* that *with* the *Mona Lisa*!

decide *on* (use with a noun): Let's *decide on* a movie.

decide *to* (use with a verb): Let's *decide to* eat out.

differ *with* (means to disagree): I *differ with* Mr. Pinkley regarding that Shakespearean sonnet.

differ *from* (means unlike): Mittens *differ from* hats because you wear mittens on your hands.

fail *in* (an attempt): I *failed in* my efforts to win first prize.

fail *to* (do something): Jeannette *failed to* submit her paper on time.

practice *for/to* (use when practice is a verb): I am *practicing for* the track meet. I have to practice to do well.

practice *of* (use when practice is a noun): The *practice of* cheating is not condoned by our school.

result *from/in* (when result is a verb): Weak fingernails *result from* not eating well. Not eating well results in weak fingernails.

result *of* (when result is a noun): This is the *result of* not eating well.

sympathy *for* (means to feel for): Brian had *sympathy for* Matt.

sympathy *with* (means agreement, sharing of feelings): Matt had *sympathy with* Brian's position in the matter.

Don't use prepositions with these, please . . .

continue: I will continue my project. Not: I will continue with my project.

inside: Paul is inside the pet house. Not: Paul is inside of the pet house.

meet: I want to meet the exchange student. Not: I want to meet with the exchange student.

name: Edwina was named best brain. Not: Edwina was named as best brain.

off: I fell off the homecoming float. Not: I fell off of the homecoming float.

visit: I am going to visit Amy this spring. Not: I am going to visit with Amy this spring.

If you are unsure, try to eliminate the offending preposition. If you can live without it, you probably don't need it.

What about ending a sentence with a preposition? You may have already heard this rule. Strictly speaking, you shouldn't end sentences with a preposition—prepositions always take an object noun, so if you don't have one after the open preposition, it is sort of left dangling there. You can correct this by rewording your sentence:

> I didn't know which house Marlene lived in.

To:

> I didn't know at which house Marlene lived.

This is one of those rules that isn't strictly followed. If you are writing a really formal paper and you absolutely don't want to have a single error, you probably should think about this rule. But, in real life, when you are speaking, if it sounds too stiff and awkward to re-word your sentences, go ahead and leave the preposition at the end. It's not really a big deal.

✍ QUIZ #34 ✍
Preposition Time

Underline the correct preposition in each of the following sentences.

1. Tom went (to, by) Michael's Pet Store yesterday.
2. You know, Tom is really very different (from, with) Michael.
3. When Tom bought that fish (off of, from) Michael, we were all very surprised.
4. (Beside, Besides) Tom, Michael doesn't have many friends.
5. (Between, Among) Michael and Tom, Tom is the more friendly.
6. Tom was upset (at, with) Michael for selling him such a boring pet.

Miscellaneous Grammar Points

Faulty Comparison

When you are comparing things, you must be sure to compare nouns to nouns and verbs to verbs. Take a look at the following sentence:

> Michelle loves Marcel more than me.

Now, what's the problem? We're comparing Michelle's love of Marcel with . . . what? That's the problem—it isn't entirely clear. Does Michelle love Marcel more than she loves the speaker here? Or, does Michelle love Marcel more than the speaker loves Marcel? In matters of grammar, as in matters of romance, you must be perfectly clear at all times. The speaker here should say either:

> Michelle loves Marcel more than I do.

Or:

> Michelle loves Marcel more than she loves me.

One more time:

> Oranges are much more wonderful to eat than apples.

Sounds fine, right? Well, this is one of those places where we all know what is meant, but still the rules of grammar have been broken. In this sentence, we are comparing *eating oranges* with *apples*. We want to compare *eating* with *eating*, so we should have said:

> Oranges are much more wonderful to eat than apples are.

Finally, remember that comparisons almost always use *like*, *as*, *than*, or *unlike*. If you use any of these words, make sure you are making a good, solid comparison.

✍ QUIZ # 35 ✍
Faulty Comparison

1. "I love Mary Ann's smile so much more than Ginger!" cried Barnaby.

   _____

   _____

2. "That may be true, but the story line on *Melrose Place* is far better than *Gilligan's Island*," shrieked Jennifer.

   _____

   _____

3. "The story line may be better, but Amanda's character is not nearly as nice as Mary Ann," answered Babette.

   _____

   _____

4. "Amanda's dresses are far more stylish than Mary Ann," offered Taylor.

   _____

   _____

5. "Perhaps, but I still think that Mary Ann's hair is much prettier than Amanda," whispered Barnaby.

   _____

   _____

Parallel Construction

If you are listing a series of things, you should make sure that they are all similar in form. For example, you may have a series of nouns:

> After going to many different movies, Ziggy realized that *character*, *plot*, and *style* were all equally important.

Not:

> After going to many different movies, Ziggy realized that *character*, *plot*, and *if there was style* were all equally important.

Do you see how the final part of the list, *style*, was changed from a noun to a clause? If you start off listing nouns, make sure all the parts of your list are nouns.

You may have a series of phrases:

> Paul hoped *to go* to college, *to get* a good job, *to go* to graduate school, and *to settle* down.

Not:

> Paul hoped *to go* to college, *to get* a good job, *to go* to graduate school and *settling down*.

Whoops! Do you hear how the direction changed at the end of that list? The first example, to go, to get, to go, and to settle, is correct because everything on the list is in the same form.

✍ QUIZ #36 ✍
Parallel Construction

Correct the error in each of the following sentences.

1. The castaways had tried many different ways to get off the island: building rafts, signaling with flares and to call ships with their radio.

   _____

   _____

2. Fred and Wilma were hosting the annual company picnic. They fried brontosaurus burgers, grilled stegosaurus ribs, and were barbecuing as well.

   _____

   _____

3. Amanda wanted to be successful, make a lot of money, and building a great empire.

   _____

   _____

4. Warning: Watching too much television can damage your brain, cause eye strain and may be interfering with your ability to read.

   _____

   _____

5. After eating, jumping rope, and to go swimming, the gang went back to its clubhouse.

   _____

   _____

Chapter 4
Punctuation

What's the point of punctuation? Take a look at these two sentences:

> Martha, my mother is the best pilot around.

> Martha, my mother, is the best pilot around.

In the first sentence, I am telling someone named Martha about my mother. In the second sentence I am telling someone about my mother, whose name is Martha. The words in each sentence are exactly the same. The punctuation changes the meaning of the sentence completely.

The thing about punctuation is that there are certain rules, many of which are open to interpretation depending on your own personal style. While you are learning, however, it's best not to fool around too much with long, strange, overly punctuated sentences. Keeping sentences relatively short and simple will keep you out of the punctuation mud for now. As you get more adventurous and confident, you can try your hand at interesting sentences filled with dashes, semicolons and commas.

THE PERIOD

Use a period in the following instances:

- When you are coming to a complete stop after a statement or a command.

    The garden around my house is very dense.

    Elvis Presley was the greatest rock and roller.

- After most abbreviations. Monograms, government organizations, television and radio networks, and post office state abbreviations don't need periods. If you have an abbreviation at the end of a sentence, you only need one period.

    Mr. Panda   V.P. Gore   etc.   a.m.

    CBS   WBCI   KZOO   CIA   JFK

- Inside parentheses if they contain a complete sentence. Put the period outside the parentheses if the words inside do not make a complete sentence.

    Mary told him (not us).

    (Mary told him.)

- Inside quotation marks.

    The sign said "Authorized Personnel Only."

- After all the letters and numbers for an outline, unless they are in parentheses:

    I.
        A.
        B.
    II.
        A.
        B.
            1.
            2.
            3.

THE COMMA

Use a comma:

- To separate two independent clauses connected by *and*, *but*, *or*, *nor*, and *for*.

  > Pierre was usually a good runner, but today he lost the race.

  > Tom was a good cook, and he always enjoyed eating what he made.

  If the clauses are short enough, you may leave out the comma.

  > Pierre won and he was happy.

  > Tom cooked and ate the fish.

- To separate items in a list. You should also put a comma before the last *and*.

  > I wanted to buy the new CDs by Green Day, Pearl Jam, and REM.

- To set off an introductory phrase from the main sentence.

  > After eating fifty-two lemon pies, Billy had quite a bad stomach ache.

  > Before leaving the party, Billy had to take some Alka-Seltzer.

- To separate a list of adjectives if you could use *and* between them.

  > The fat, sickly, ugly, smelly baboon was sitting in the corner.

  > (You could say "The fat and sickly and ugly and smelly baboon . . .")

- To separate the name of a person you are addressing, or a person's title.

  > That is why, Mr. Smithers, Dagwood won't be at work today.

  > Mr. Smithers, Dagwood's boss, is quite upset about the budget.

- To set off a group of words that contrast with what you are saying.

  > I like to swim, not dive, when I go to the pool.

  > Alice was going to sing, not dance, at the talent show.

- To set apart the figures in a date, and the parts of an address (not between the state and the zip code, however).

  > May 15, 1996

  > 35 Rosewood Street, Cleveland, OH 00001

- To separate hundreds, thousands, millions, and every three digits thereafter.

  > 1,876,967,300

- To avoid confusion in a sentence. That's the main purpose of a comma, after all. If you need to pause, or set aside a group of words to make your meaning clear, use a comma. Try not to overdo it.

  > After waking up, my sister ate breakfast.

Not:

  > After waking up my sister ate breakfast.

The Question Mark

Use a question mark as follows:

- To show that a direct question is being asked.

  Do you want to go to Michael's Pet Store with me?

  You don't need a question mark for an indirect question.

  She wanted to know if he would be going to the pet store with her.

- Put the question mark inside quotation marks if the quotation is a question. Put the question mark outside the quotation marks if the quote itself is not a question.

  "Would you like some of this fish?"
  (The quote is a question.)

  Do you know who said, "Give me liberty or give me death"?
  (The quote is not a question.)

The Exclamation Point

Use an exclamation point:

- If you are expressing a strong statement or sentiment.

  I really love that movie!

- To set off an interjection for emphasis.

  Yikes! That fire is hot.

- But don't overuse exclamation points. People use them way too much. Try to limit the use of exclamation points to strong feelings and statements, or your writing will look silly. Take a look at these two examples:

  The Pineview Eagles have been having their best year ever! Star quarterback David Barzinski did a great job this past Saturday! He scored two touchdowns! It was a great game! Go, Eagles!

Or:

> The Pineview Eagles have been having their best
> year ever. Star quarterback David Barzinski did
> a great job this past Saturday. He scored two
> touchdowns. It was a great game. Go, Eagles!

The first sample makes the reader feel as if she is being
yelled at. It also loses punch after awhile. So, try to keep
your use of exclamation points to a minimum, and never
use two or more in the same place.

THE SEMICOLON

Semicolons are tricky, and many people don't use them
correctly. Here are the rules:

- Use a semicolon when two independent clauses are
  not joined by a conjunction. If you can separate the
  parts into two separate sentences, you can use a
  semicolon.

  > Marlene felt that the fish was overcooked; the
  > dinner was wonderful other than that.

  > The test results came in; Georgette was the clear
  > leader.

- Use a semicolon if you have a long list of names
  which already includes commas. In this case commas would not clearly separate the names, so use
  semicolons instead.

  > We were soon joined by Prof. Elizabeth Young-
  > Smith, head of the English Department, from
  > Middle Valley, Ohio; Dean Jane Farfetch, team
  > leader, from West Hills, Indiana; and Ms. Petra
  > Mustang, Social Studies lead teacher, from South
  > Eastville, Michigan.

The Colon

A colon is used:

- To introduce a list.

   The problems were always the same on the island: floods, volcanoes, and monsoons.

- To introduce a long quote.

   It was John F. Kennedy who said: "Ask not what your country can do for you; ask what you can do for your country."

- To introduce an explanation.

   There are many reasons for our coming here: we wanted to meet Michael, and we were interested in purchasing a new pet.

Quotation Marks

Use quotation marks in the following instances:

- Around a direct quote. Put any commas or periods inside the quotation marks. Put question marks and exclamation marks inside the quotation marks only if they are part of the quote; put them outside if they are not.

   "Let's get going," said Jane "or we'll be late."

   "Don't you want to go?" asked Chris.

   "Look at me!" cried Barnaby.

   I don't think Mr. Smith knows we call him "Mr. Fatso"!

   Do you know why Mom said "we are not going"?

- To set off a statement that is the opposite of what you really mean. Only use quotation marks this way if it is absolutely necessary, or your writing will look too silly.

Michelle "borrowed" my homework so that she could copy it.

- If quotations are longer than one paragraph, you should put new quotation marks at the beginning of each new paragraph, but only at the end of the last paragraph.

> "I went to the beach one day this summer. It was quite beautiful and sunny. The day was really picture perfect.
>
> "Then, to my surprise, a giant thundercloud passed over the sun. It began to rain. The day was completely ruined."

- You don't need quotation marks for an indirect quote.

> He told us that he would be happy to join us at the party.
>
> She said thank you to all her guests.

THE DASH

Dashes are optional. Some people love to use dashes—others don't.

- You may wish to use dashes like commas, to set off a phrase.

> She was quite a sight—all done up and wearing that new dress—for her sweet sixteen party.

- You may substitute dashes for parentheses.

> When you come to the party—this Saturday night—bring lots of tortilla chips and guacamole.
>
> Instead of:
>
> When you come to the party (this Saturday night) bring lots of tortilla chips and guacamole.

PARENTHESES

Parentheses are used as follows:

- To set off any extra words that would otherwise interrupt your sentence.

  > Max (wonder dog extraordinaire) was perform-
  > ing at the local talent show.

- Put a period inside the parentheses if they contain a complete sentence. Otherwise, put the period outside the parentheses. Don't put a comma after the parentheses unless you would use one anyway.

  > We wanted to go to the show (without Sam).

✍ QUIZ #37 ✍
Anna Banana, We're Home!

Punctuate the following paragraph. Remember that there is some flexibility here, but do your best and try to keep the paragraph clear.

Barnaby Babette Sondra Taylor and Jennifer were all quite tired but exhilarated nonetheless The Professor was not quite as smart as I'd always hoped but it was neat to finally see him anyway Barnaby said

Maybe you're right about the Professor said Jennifer but no one could compare to Amanda and her amazing clothes Are you kidding She was so mean said Taylor

I think we all had some pretty exciting adventures said Jennifer but I for one am happy to be back here All that fighting and drama has worn me out

Yes agreed Taylor I don't think I would really want to be in The Brady Bunch after all

I would definitely not want to be a part of the stupid Dylan's Beverly Hills show said Babette I am very glad to be home

The gang soon realized one thing being part of a television show would be pretty exhausting after a while Let's burn that ticket said Taylor It's the only safe reasonable thing to do

I think he is right said Barnaby Logically speaking of course we should cut our losses and just hang here despite the great heat

They made a ceremonial fire and watched the silver ticket crumple and burn

There's no place like home cried Bridget

Chapter 5

The Princeton Review List of Commonly Misused and Confused Words

LEARNING TO SPELL CORRECTLY

It seems that some people are naturally good spellers and others just aren't. To a degree that's true. Some people have a knack for spotting misspelled words. Good spelling is not just about memorizing rules and words; it's a matter of recognizing words. In fact, good spelling often means learning to spot a misspelled word—not necessarily knowing how to spell every word.

Does that seem strange? Good spellers don't automatically know how to spell everything, but they do recognize a word that is misspelled. To them, misspellings just look funny. How do you cultivate this talent? There are two steps:

1. **Reading** is probably the best way to train yourself to recognize misspelled words. Why? Well, the more you look at words that are spelled correctly

(and let's assume that in most books the words *are* spelled correctly) the more you recognize wrongly spelled words. It's like eating in good restaurants all the time—after a while, you start to know the difference between good food and bad food.

2. **Edit** your own work. Get in the habit of rereading your work before you hand it in. Circle or mark any words that look even remotely wrong to you. How many can you spot? If you are using a computer, try to check for misspellings before you use the spell checker. Now, it would be really great if you looked up all those words, but right now, the first step is to train yourself to recognize words that look wrong.

Now what?

You're soon going to notice which words you always misspell. It's just a bad habit. Do you have some rule in your head like "i before e except after c" and as a result you always spell weird "wierd"? That's understandable. Now you're going to look at the words you misspell and think up a mnemonic to remember how to spell them.

What's a mnemonic?

A **mnemonic** (new MAHN ik) is a little memory device. "I before e except after c" is a spelling mnemonic. But there are other ways to remember the correct spelling.

Look at the part of the word you always misspell. For example, sep*e*rate is a common misspelling. Now look at the right way to spell that word: sep*a*rate. Check out the spot in the word that gives you trouble. Almost everybody puts an "e" instead of an "a" in the middle. So, in order to remember the correct spelling, you may say to yourself: "There's *a rat* in separate."

And what about weird? You may just remember that "weird is weird" so it doesn't follow the rules.

What if I can't think up a mnemonic?

If you really can't think up a mnemonic, we're willing to bet you memorized the spelling of the word just by thinking about it so hard. Many times it helps to sound out the word **phonetically** (meaning that you would pronounce it in your head exactly the way it is spelled) if it has a strange spelling. For example, you might say the phrase "to get her" to yourself whenever you spell "together."

Don't use silly spellings when you write!

We have to put a plea in for this—don't write using fun, silly spellings of words such as *nite* (instead of night), *thru* (instead of through) or, most importantly, *luv* (instead of love). These may be okay for notes to your friends, but you should never use them in any formal writing assignment.

Commonly misspelled words

achievement	i before e except after c
believe	i before e except after c
committee	2 m's, 2 t's, 2 e's
definite	no a—just 2 i's in definite
dependent/ independent	you don't need to be dependent to get a dent
occasion	2 c's, but only one s in occasion
occurred	2 c's, 2 r's
parallel	there are 2 parallel l's in the middle
pleasant	there's an ant in pleasant
receive	i before e, except after c
recommend	one c, 2 m's in recommend
referring	one f only in referring
separate	there's a rat in separate

DICTION

Diction means word choice. Using the right word at the right time not only shows how brilliantly you speak and write, but it makes your speaking and writing clearer and more precise. If you use the wrong word, people will think your speech or writing is sloppy, or they may misunderstand your meaning. The following list of words are among those most commonly misused. You hear many of them used incorrectly every day.

The Offending Words

Absolutely
Do you mean *yes*? If you're writing, better to use the simpler, more direct word.

Affect/Effect
Affect is a verb. It means to influence. You can *affect* the situation you are in. Your teacher can *affect* your grade in English. Your mother can *affect* your ideas about life.

Effect is usually a noun, meaning the result. The *effect* was stunning. The special *effect* in the movie was spectacular.

Effect can sometimes be used as a verb as well—if it is, it means to accomplish. The new principal hoped to *effect* a number of changes in the school.

Aggravate/Irritate
You *aggravate* a situation. You *irritate* a person. *Aggravate* means to make something worse. So, if your mother tells you that you're *aggravating* her, you can tell her that, no, in fact, you are *irritating* her. Won't that do the trick? Tommy was so *irritated* by his aunt's frequent nagging about his hair. The skin rash was *aggravated* by the lotion she put on.

Agree to/Agree with
You agree *to* something and *with* someone. Helen *agreed with* John. They *agreed to* stop fighting for just one day.

Ain't

Ain't no such word. Use *isn't*. There *isn't* any reason for you to do poorly on the test.

Allusion/Illusion

When you refer to something indirectly, that's an allusion. An illusion is that rabbit out of a hat sort of thing. Her speech was sprinkled with *allusions* to all the famous people she had met. Making the Statue of Liberty disappear was one of David Copperfield's greatest *illusions*.

Alot/A lot

You say *a little*, right? So why are you making *a lot* into one word? There *is* no word *alot*. She had *a lot* of reasons not to do her homework.

All together/Altogether

All together means together as a group. *Altogether* means completely. We were *all together* this year for Thanksgiving. You are *altogether* right about that one!

Among/Between

Use *among* when you are talking about more than two things. Use *between* only when referring to two things. If you have two groups, you may also use *between*, even though there may be a lot of people in each group. The slimy fight *between* the citizens of Butterville and Margarinetown continued for many years. *Between* you and me, that was the worst fish I've ever eaten. *Among* the students in Ms. Ella's class, Ida Mae was the best.

As/Like

Use *as* when you are comparing phrases, and *like* when you are comparing nouns and pronouns. She's almost as smart *as* I am. He's just *like* his brother.

Basically

Avoid this word whenever you can. It's not technically wrong, but it is overused. Often you don't need it at all. Instead of "Basically, I'm in it for the money," you can just say, "I'm in it for the money."

Being that/Being as

These sound pretentious. Remember that the point is to be clear and precise. Just say *because*. *Because* I want to do well, I am avoiding silly-sounding phrases.

Beside/Besides

Beside means *next to*. *Besides* means *in addition to*. Try not to mix them up. "I was hoping to sit *beside* Jake," Sydney said. You have a lot to worry about *besides* Amanda.

Between you and . . . ?

Okay, once and for all: the correct phrase is *between you and me*, not between you and I. Remember that *between* is a preposition, so it always takes an object pronoun. *Between you and me*, this is the most delicious slop I've ever eaten.

Bring/Take

You *bring* things to the person who is speaking. You *take* things away from the person who is speaking. *Bring* me the head of John the Baptist! Calgon—*take* me away! "*Take* this tray to your mother," said Dad. "*Bring* me the tray!" yelled Mom.

Borrow/Lend

Same idea as above: you *borrow* from someone; you *lend* to someone. May I *borrow* your book? I'll *lend* it to you.

Can/May

People almost always use *can* when they mean *may*. Asking if you *can* leave the room is asking if you have the ability to leave the room. Use *can* if you want to know if you are able to do something. Use *may* if you want to ask for permission. "*Can* I eat 280 cherry pies?" wondered Beatrice. "*May* I watch her try?" asked Beatrice's sister, Lilly.

Can't hardly

Hardly is a negative word. If you can't hardly, then you can. What you want to say is *can hardly*. The same is true for *can barely*. I *can barely* keep my eyes open. I *can hardly* wait for my birthday.

Compare/Contrast

You *compare* things when you bring them together to talk about their points of similarity and difference. If you are *contrasting* things, you are only looking at how they are different from each other. The teacher asked us to *compare* the characters in the books we are reading. The *contrast* between Ms. Hoffmeyer and Mr. Zinger is striking—she is so laid back and he is so tense!

Compare with/Compare to

Compare with is generally used when you have two equal things and you want to point out differences. *Compare to* is used to point out similarities. *Compared with* Mr. Wylie's class, Ms. Smith's is a breeze! Shall I *compare* thee *to* a summer's day?

Complement/Compliment

To *complement* with an *e* means to go together with. To *compliment* with an *i* means to say nice things about. You can remember the difference by thinking that *I* like to receive *compliments*. Spaghetti *complements* meatballs so perfectly. Mr. Smyth *complimented* my use of perfect grammar.

Could of

Is always wrong. The right thing to say is *could have*. The same holds true for *would of* or *should of*. I *could have* been a contender!

Further/Farther

Farther refers to time and quantity measurements. Use *further* to mean *more*. He couldn't go any *farther* on the trail after he sprained his ankle. Laurice wanted to have *further* discussion about the new rules.

Fewer/Less

Fewer refers to things that can be counted. *Less* refers to a general quantity. This one's fun, because you can catch many teachers asking for "five pages or *less*," when they should be asking for "five pages or *fewer*." How about those express lines at the supermarket? How many signs can you spot that say "ten items or *less*"? (That's wrong!) I'd like *fewer* french fries and *less* mashed potatoes. Give me *fewer* egg rolls and *less* soup.

Former/Latter

Former refers to the first of two things and *latter* refers to the second, or last of the two. You can remember these because *former* begins with an "*f*" just like first and *latter* begins with an "*l*" just like last. Money and health: the *former* can make you comfortable, but only the *latter* can make you feel good.

Goes

Do you mean *says*? If you say things like, "So, she goes, 'Get outta here!'" then stop it! Don't say *goes* unless you are talking about someone going somewhere. If you are telling someone what someone else said, use the right word, *says*. So, Mary Ann *says*, "Get out of my face!"

Healthful/Healthy

If you lead a *healthful* life, you will be *healthy*. *Healthful* refers to something that gives you health or leads to good health. People, plants, and animals can be *healthy*. Diet, climates, and exercise programs can be *healthful*. I stopped eating potato chips and now I feel so *healthy*. But my new *healthful* life is just no fun.

Hopefully

People misuse this word all the time. *Hopefully* means *with hope*. You wait *hopefully* for the results of your test, for example (meaning that you are waiting with hope). Technically you shouldn't say "Hopefully, we will come here tomorrow" unless you mean that you will all come here tomorrow "with hope." The easy way out of this is to use *I hope* when you are writing: *I hope* to do well on my exam. *Hopefully* is so widely misused that it is becoming acceptable, especially in speech.

Imply/Infer

If you *imply* something, you are hinting at it. You *infer* something when you figure it out. If your father *implies* that you need a haircut, you might *infer* that he doesn't like your style. Mr. Katzenjammer *implied* that we would have a pop quiz tomorrow. Marjorie *inferred* from Joe's nervous behavior that he liked her.

Immigrate/Emigrate

To *immigrate* is to move to a new country. You *emigrate* from the country you are leaving. Think of the *immigrants*—they were coming to the United States. The *immigrants* of the early 1900s flocked through Ellis Island. They *emigrated* from Ireland during the great Potato Famine.

In regards to

Use *regarding* or *in regard to* (no *s*). *Regarding* your letter, I will be there on the 14th.

Intelligent/Intelligible

Intelligent means smart. If something is *intelligible*, it is understandable. Lionel's speech was *intelligent*; he made references to all the books in our course. Rose's speech was *intelligible*; she spoke clearly and loudly.

Irregardless

No such word. Say *regardless*. *Regardless* of what you think, I am going to dye my hair green.

It's/Its

It's is a contraction meaning *it is*. We know it's confusing, but *its* is the possessive form of the pronoun *it*. Remember that none of the possessive pronouns take *–'s*. Think of his, hers, theirs, ours—none of them have an *–'s*. *It's* so difficult to keep all these chairs straight. That chair is broken; *its* leg is cracked in the middle.

Lay/Lie

These are confusing. Check out the section on weird verbs (page 64). *Lay* means to set down. *Lie* means to recline. *Lay* the book on the table. *Lie* on the couch.

Many/Much

Same as fewer/less. Use *many* for things that can be counted and *much* for a general quantity. *Many* of the people at the party were pigs. *Much* of the dip was gone by the time I got to the buffet table.

Most

Be careful not to use this word when you mean *almost.* Don't say, "*Most* everyone was there." *Almost* everyone was there.

Nauseated/Nauseous

Most people say *nauseous* when they mean *nauseated.* If you are *nauseous*, you make someone sick. If you are *nauseated*, you feel sick. If something is *nauseous*, it makes you *nauseated.* The smell of rotten eggs is *nauseous.* She was *nauseated* by the idea of eating the pet fish.

Number/Amount

Same as fewer/less. *Number* refers to things that can be counted. *Amount* refers to a quantity of things that cannot be counted separately. I have a *number* of dollars in my wallet. The *amount* of money she spends is mind-blowing! The *number* of eggs in the recipe was reduced. The *amount* of milk was increased.

Persecuted/Prosecuted

If you *persecute* someone you annoy them excessively. To *prosecute* means to be brought before a court of law. I think Ms. Happy is trying to *persecute* me with all this homework! This country believes that criminals should be *prosecuted* for their crimes.

Principle/Principal

The *principal* of your school is your pal—it ends in *pal.* Principal also functions as an adjective meaning "most important."

A *principle* is a rule or a guideline. The *principal* reason *Principal* Green was there was to help out. His *principles* inspire him to help people.

Respectively/Respectfully

Respectively means in that order. *Respectfully* means with respect. Some people sign letters *"respectfully* yours." The most important things in life are health, happiness, and money, *respectively*. I submit this application to you *respectfully*.

Snuck

No way! The correct past tense form of sneak is *sneaked*: She *sneaked* down the hall, past her sleeping parents, and off to the party.

Stationary/Stationery

Remember that *stationery* with an *e* goes into an envelope (which starts with *e*) and is sold in a *stationery* store. *Stationary* with an *a* means staying still: The spider remained *stationary* for hours, waiting for its prey. Our local *stationery* store sells the prettiest blue *stationery*.

Too/To

Too is an adverb meaning *also* or *more than enough*. *To* is a preposition—use it to place a noun: We are going *to* my house after dinner. You are *too* much!

Ultimate

Use *ultimate* to mean *final*. Don't use ultimate to mean the best, as in the "ultimate taste sensation!" You'll sound like a commercial. They finally reached their *ultimate* destination—home.

You're/Your

People get this one wrong all the time. *You're* is a contraction meaning *you are*. *Your* is the possessive form of the pronoun *you*. *You're* invited to the party! *Your* puppy is so cute.

Diction

Underline the correct word in each of the following sentences.

1. After returning from her adventures, Bridget was so tired, she was barely (intelligent, intelligible).

2. We need to buy some paper from the (stationary, stationery) store and write all this down.

3. ("Your, You're) kidding, right?" said Barnaby. "(Its, It's) (to, too) unbelievable."

4. "That stupid ticket sure was (aggravating, irritating). We hardly had (none, any) good luck," growled Jennifer.

5. "If we had (fewer, less) adventures, we wouldn't have anything fun to talk about," Sondra pointed out.

6. "We should have (snuck, sneaked) past Dylan and gone to find Brandon," Babette pouted.

7. "Well, I am going to (lay, lie) down now and take a nap. That was exhausting," Barnaby said.

The School of Redundancy School

A redundancy occurs when you repeat yourself, or use words that are not necessary. The following phrases are redundant. Try to avoid using them.

4 a.m. in the morning—a.m. means *in the morning*. p.m. means *at night*. Don't say *9 p.m. at night* either.

At this point in time—Just say "at this time," or how about plain old "now"?

An approximate guess—You either approximate or you guess. Same thing.

Believe you me—When you say "Believe me," the *you* is implied, so you don't need to include it.

Both alike—If you say simply "They are alike," you don't need the both.

Circle around—If you are circling, you are going around.

Consensus of opinion—Just say consensus. If you have a consensus, you have a whole bunch of opinions working together. The *consensus* was that Mr. Geekly was the worst teacher in the school.

Dead corpse—A *corpse* is *dead*. But you knew that, didn't you?

Estimated at about—Say either "about" or "estimated at." The student body is *estimated at* 300. There are *about* 300 students in our school.

He is a man who/She is a woman who—Too many words. All you need to say is "He is . . ." or "She is . . ."

Pair of twins—Avoid this, unless you mean four people.

The reason is because—Say "the reason is . . ." or "because . . ." *The reason* I want to finish this book *is* that I need to write a book report. I want to finish this book *because* I have to write a book report.

Too premature, too perfect, really pregnant, very unique—These things either are or aren't. You can't have varying degrees of them. You are either *premature* or you're not. You are either *perfect* or you're not. Well, you get the idea.

The year of 1995—Just say 1995.

True fact—A fact is true. All you need to say is *fact*.

Glossary

active voice: when the subject acts directly (as compared to the passive voice, when things happen to the subject). (*Mary drove to the store.*)

adjective: a word that describes a noun or a pronoun (*beautiful, smart, nice, happy*).

adverb: a word that describes a verb, an adjective, or another adverb. Adverbs often, but not always, end in *-ly* (*quickly, very, nicely*).

agreement: a term used either to indicate that the subject must agree with the verb (*he smiles* instead of *he smile*) or that the pronoun must agree with the noun it replaces. (*The people want their hamburgers* instead of *The people want his hamburger.*)

appositive: a noun or pronoun, set off by commas, that explains something. (John, *my best friend*, is getting me tickets to the concert.)

apostrophe: a punctuation mark that shows ownership (*Mark's bicycle*) or a contraction (*don't, won't*).

article: *the, a,* and *an* are articles. They are short words used to tell *which one.*

case: category that shows the function of a pronoun. The subjective (or nominative) case pronoun is used for the *subject* of a sentence. The objective case is used for the *object* of a sentence.

clause: a group of words with a subject and a verb. Independent clauses may stand alone; dependent clauses may not.

collective noun: a group noun, which is usually treated as singular (*audience, jury, government*).

colon: punctuation mark used to introduce a list or an example. (*We need two things: courage and patience.*)

comma: punctuation mark used for a pause, or to set off part of a sentence for clarity.

conjunction: joining word. May act alone or in pairs. *And, but,* and *or* are conjunctions that act alone. *Neither . . . nor, either . . . or,* and *not only . . . but* are conjunctions that work in pairs.

dash: a punctuation mark that may be used like a comma or parentheses. (*You know—don't you—that I really like to skate.*)

demonstrative pronoun: a pronoun used to indicate which thing you are talking about (*that, these, those, this*).

dependent clause: a group of words with a subject and a verb that would not make sense standing alone as a sentence. (The boy told us *he would come and play baseball.*)

diction: correct word choice.

direct object: the noun that receives the action in the sentence. (I want to eat *hamburgers.*)

future: tense used to indicate something that will happen. Uses the words *will* or *shall.*

future perfect: tense used to show an action that will be finished before a specific time in the future. (Before next Wednesday, I *will have* lost five pounds.)

gender: applies to nouns and pronouns that refer to people. It can either be male, female, or neutral (applying to both men and women).

gerund: -ing form of a verb, which acts as a noun. (*Skating* is great.)

helping verb: the second or third verbs used with the main verb if the verb is more than one word. (We *will* go to the park. I *have been* trying not to eat ice cream.)

idiom: the way we put words together, even if it doesn't literally make sense or follow any specific rule. Idioms include funny expressions (*Let a smile be your umbrella.*) and preposition use (A foot is *different from* a meter.).

indefinite pronoun: a pronoun that doesn't stand for a particular noun. *Each, either, any, few, none, some* are indefinite pronouns. Make sure they are in agreement when you use them.

independent clause: the main clause of the sentence. It can stand alone, without the dependent clauses. (*The boy told us* he would come and play baseball.)

indirect object: receiver of the direct object. Can be turned into a prepositional phrase. (Give *me* your skates.)

infinitive: the "to" form of the verb (*to be, to go, to eat).*

interjection: an introductory word, used for emphasis. (*Cool! Yikes! Wow! Hey!*)

interrogative pronoun: a pronoun used to ask a question. (*Who? What? Which?*)

misplaced modifier: a phrase or word that is not next to the thing it is modifying. It makes sentences unclear.

modify: describe. Adjectives and adverbs are modifiers.

nominative case: also called subjective case. The pronoun used for the subject of the verb.

noun: a person, place, thing or idea (*book, house, truth, love*).

number: whether something is singular or plural.

object: the object of a verb is the thing acted upon by the subject. (I ate *ice cream*.) The object of a preposition is the noun that is being placed by the preposition. (We went to *the house*.)

objective case: the form of pronoun used as the object of a verb.

parallel construction: the rule that when you construct a list, all the things in the list should be in the same form.

participle: the present participle of a verb is the *-ing* form and goes with *is* (*is going, is eating*). The past participle usually ends in *-ed* and goes with *have* (*have asked, have gone*).

past tense: the tense that indicates that something has already happened. The past tense is most commonly used for story-telling.

past perfect: the past before the past. (Before I went to the store, I *had gone* to the dance.)

period: punctuation mark used at the end of a statement sentence, or for abbreviations.

person: the term used to categorize personal pronouns. *First person* refers to the speaker: I, we. *Second person* refers to the person being spoken to: you. *Third person* refers to the person being spoken about: he, she, they.

phrase: a group of words that work together as one part of speech in a sentence, but do not have both a subject and a verb. The main types of phrases are prepositional, infinitive, participial, and gerund.

plural: more than one, as opposed to singular. Nouns, pronouns, and verbs may be plural or singular.

possessive pronoun: pronoun which shows ownership (*my, his, hers, its, theirs*).

predicate: the part of the sentence that is not the subject. The predicate includes the verb and all descriptive phrases.

preposition: a word used to place a noun in time or space (*at, toward, around, before, into, after*).

present tense: tense used to show that something is happening right now, or to state a fact.

present perfect: tense used to show an action that began in the past, but continues into the present, or was finished at some earlier time. (I *have lost* fifteen pounds.)

principal parts: the basic forms of the verb that are used for the different tenses. The principal parts include the present, past, and past participle.

pronoun: a word that stands in for a noun (*he, she, it, they*).

question mark: punctuation mark used at the end of a question. (*How are you?*)

quotation mark: punctuation marks used to show a quote. (*"How are you?" asked Jennifer.*)

redundancy: saying the same thing twice; using unnecessary words.

reflexive pronoun: is used to refer to the subject. (*He ate it himself.* Or, for emphasis: *I, myself, love pizza.*)

semicolon: punctuation mark used to separate independent clauses. (*I came; I saw; I conquered.*)

singular: refers to nouns and pronouns when there is only one, as opposed to two or more. Singular is also used to refer to the verb that goes with a singular noun or pronoun.

subject: the noun or pronoun that performs the action in the sentence.

tense: the form of the verb that tells when the action happened. The six main tenses are: present, present perfect, past, past perfect, future, and future perfect.

verb: a word that expresses an action or a state of being. You must have a verb to have a sentence (*run, jump, seem, think*).

verbal: a phrase that contains a word that looks like a verb, but doesn't act like a verb. The three main types of verbals are gerunds (*skating*), infinitives (*to sing*), and participles (*singing*).

Answers

✍ QUIZ #1 ✍
What's this Ticket?

Underline the common nouns and circle the proper nouns in the following passage.

It was a hot <u>day</u> around the old <u>clubhouse</u>.(Sondra)(Barnaby,) (Babette,)(Taylor)(Bridget) and (Jennifer) had been hanging around watching <u>television</u> most of that <u>week</u>—it seemed too hot to do anything else.

"<u>Man</u>, what I wouldn't do to spend a <u>week</u> on (Gilligan's) (Island.)" said (Barnaby.) "First of all, I wouldn't mind meeting the (Professor,) and secondly, it sure would be nice and cool there."

"Forget (Gilligan's Island,)" answered (Jennifer.) "Give me (Melrose Place) any <u>day</u>. I'd love to hang with (Amanda,) meet (Jake,) bum around with that whole <u>gang</u>. Their <u>lives</u> sure seem exciting."

"You <u>guys</u> are weird." said (Taylor) dreamily. "Give me a nice happy <u>family</u> like the (Brady Bunch.) Now there are some fun <u>people</u> I'd like to spend a <u>week</u> with."

"What's this <u>ticket</u> on the <u>floor</u>?" asked (Bridget.) "I've never seen anything like it before."

✍ QUIZ #2 ✍
A Ticket to Adventure

Underline the pronouns in the following passage.

"<u>It</u> says, '<u>This</u> is <u>your</u> ticket to adventure. If <u>you</u> hold tightly onto <u>it</u>, <u>you</u> will be transported to the place of <u>your</u> dreams. To escape from <u>your</u> adventure, say the words *anna banana*,'" said Jennifer.

"That's strange. What do you suppose it means?" wondered Babette.

"I suppose that it means exactly what it says. Where would we like to go?" answered Barnaby, logical as usual.

"Me, I would like to go to Melrose Place," laughed Jennifer, picking up the ticket.

"That seems like a weird place to me." said Taylor.

But it was too late. The clubhouse began to rattle. They all held onto the nearest piece of furniture. Before you could say "Sydney," they were off.

✍ QUIZ #3 ✍
Melrose Place, Here We Come!

Underline the verbs in the following passage.

Jennifer opened the door slowly. The pool glimmered in the mid-afternoon sun. Soon, she heard a familiar voice screech into the silence.

"What is this disgustingly ugly house doing around my pool?" yelled Amanda.

"Uh, we are not exactly sure ourselves," answered Jennifer. "Is this really Melrose Place?

"You bet, sweetie," answered Amanda. "And if you don't hightail this broken down old clubhouse from our private pool, you will live to regret your visit here."

"Amanda, what is the problem?" Jake entered the scene.

"No problem, sweetie. Just a bunch of rude, noisy kids trespassing on our property. I am sure they will find a way out of here before you can wink an eye." Amanda turned on her heel, stomped into the apartment, and slammed the door behind her.

"Hmm, what do you think of Amanda now?" asked Sondra.

"Ugh," answered Jennifer. "Anna banana."

✍ QUIZ #4 ✍

Just Sit Right Back and You'll Hear a Tale . . .

Underline the adjectives in the following passage.

The clubhouse may have been <u>shabby</u>, but it was <u>sturdy</u> enough to get them back home in a wink.

"Wow," said Jennifer, "this <u>silver</u> ticket really works! We should think hard about the next <u>exciting</u> place we'd like to go."

"We could go somewhere <u>cool</u>," offered Barnaby.

"Somewhere <u>fun</u>," said Babette.

"Somewhere <u>exotic</u>," said Taylor.

"Hmm, Melrose Place wasn't <u>exotic</u> enough for you?" asked a <u>nervous</u> Bridget. She snapped her <u>cherry</u> gum and blew an <u>enormous</u> bubble.

"No, let's try someplace <u>new</u> and <u>different</u>," answered Babette.

"Someplace where there are <u>cool ocean</u> breezes, perhaps?" asked Barnaby.

"Yeah, <u>cool, fresh</u> breezes. That sounds pretty <u>nice</u>." Taylor looked off into the <u>steamy</u> street.

"Maybe Gilligan's Island?" Barnaby grabbed the <u>silver</u> ticket and rubbed it.

✍ QUIZ #5 ✍

The Professor and Barnaby

Underline the adverbs in the following passage.

"Gilligan!" yelled Mary Ann. She ran <u>breathlessly</u> up the beach and into the woods. The kids were perched <u>clumsily</u> in the nearest coconut tree.

"What's the matter Mary Ann? You seem <u>very</u> upset." Gilligan ran <u>quickly</u> to her.

"No, it's just that I heard something—a <u>very</u> funny kind of crash. I'm a little scared, Gilligan. Let's go get the Professor."

"The Professor!" whispered Barnaby, <u>excitedly</u>. "I have <u>always</u> wanted to meet him. One of the great minds of sitcom land."

"Sure, if he's <u>so</u> <u>very</u> smart, how come he <u>never</u> got them off this stupid island?" Bridget snapped her gum <u>furiously</u>.

"Sssh, Bridget, here he comes!" Barnaby pointed at the figure moving <u>slowly</u> through the clump of trees.

"Professor, we're <u>really</u> stuck. Here! Up in this tree!" called Barnaby.

"My, my, how did you kids get stuck up in a coconut tree?" pondered the Professor. "And who are you, anyway? How can we be sure that you aren't a bunch of spies, sent here by some of our enemies?"

"Spies? Professor, I am your <u>very</u> biggest fan," cried Barnaby."

"Oh, <u>really</u>?" asked the Professor. "And how is it that you know my name?"

✍ QUIZ #6 ✍
Court Martial on Gilligan's Island

Circle the prepositions in the following passage.

Once (in) the hut, the kids began to panic. "How did we get ourselves (into) this?" asked Taylor.

"Don't worry—I'll get us out (of) this trouble." Barnaby was confident. "I can reason (with) the Professor."

"Okay, kids, we don't know who you are, but we suspect you are a bunch (of) spies. How else would you all know our names?" said the Skipper pacing (around) the room as he spoke.

"I can prove we're not spies!" cried Babette. "I don't know anything (about) this stupid show! I only watch *Beverly Hills 90210*."

"A likely story!" answered Ginger. "I've been (to) Beverly Hills, of course, and I'm sure it would be very boring to just sit and watch it all day long. Only a spy would do that! They're trying to learn all (of) our customs."

"Let's feed them (to) the crocodiles!" yelled Mary Ann.

"No, let's send them out (on) a raft!" countered the Professor.

"Forget it!" Barnaby rolled his eyes. "*Anna banana*."

Wilma!

Underline the conjunctions in the following passage.

"Ugh," Barnaby rolled his eyes <u>as</u> they landed back at home. "<u>Neither</u> Melrose Place <u>nor</u> Gilligan's Island was at all what I'd imagined."

"Maybe we'd better forget all about this ticket <u>and</u> traveling for today." Bridget snapped her gum.

"<u>Not only</u> are you guys boring, <u>but</u> you also lack imagination," Sondra said. "Let's go someplace, I don't know, unreal. How about Bedrock?"

"Where?" asked Taylor. He had never heard of Melrose Place <u>or</u> Bedrock. This was beginning to tire him out.

"You know—Fred, Wilma, Betty, <u>and</u> Barney. Bedrock!"

"Barney? You mean that large purple dinosaur? I don't think so!" Babette wrinkled her nose <u>and</u> threw her hands up in disgust.

"Not Barney the purple dinosaur, Babette, Barney from the cartoon The Flintstones. C'mon, <u>either</u> you give me that ticket <u>or</u> I'll never speak to you again."

"Here—do what you want—I give up." Barnaby tossed the ticket at Sondra's feet.

"Wilma—I always wanted to meet you <u>and</u> Betty." Sondra rubbed the ticket. The walls of the clubhouse began to shimmer. The kids felt weird <u>and</u> wobbly. They were turning into cartoon characters!

We Forgot About the Dinosaurs

Ha! Find the interjections! Underline them!

"<u>Heh</u>! Barney," called Fred. "Check this out."

"What is it Fred?" Barney leaned over the stone fence between their houses. "<u>Yikes</u>! What's that, Fred?"

"I'm not sure Barn—it looks like some kind of strange wooden house. Who ever heard of a wooden house?"

The kids nervously peered out the window.

"_Cool_! We're cartoons. Look, Sondra, there's Fred and Barney. They're pointing at us. Wave."

"_Heh_, you kids. What are you doing in our tree? _Wilma_! Call the Rock Police!"

"_Oh_!" Wilma walked out into the yard. "What's going on here, Fred?"

Dino came bounding into the yard. "_Yip, yip_!" He jumped up at the base of the tree, clawing furiously at the bottom of the clubhouse.

"They don't seem very friendly, either," Sondra shook her head.

"_Oh, well_, anna banana."

Chapter 1 Review

There are _eight_ parts of speech. Can you name them? Give a quick definition and an example of each one.

1. **noun:** names a person, place, thing, or idea
   book, story, love, justice, truth, cat, dog, fish

2. **pronoun:** takes the place of a noun
   he, she, it, they, their, its, mine, myself

3. **verb:** describes action or state of being
   run, dance, seem, appear, think, is, were

4. **adjective:** describes a noun or pronoun
   ugly, pretty, nice, small, big

5. **adverb:** describes a verb, adjective, or another adverb
   quickly, nicely, fast, very, so

6. **preposition:** places a noun in time or space
   after, before, in, to, out, from, over

7. **conjunction:** joins together parts of a sentence

8. **interjection:** exclamation word used for emphasis
   hah!, yikes!, cool!

Use *N* for noun, *P* for pronoun, *V* for verb, *ADJ* for adjective, *ADV* for adverb, *PR* for preposition, *C* for conjunction and *I* for interjection.

1. Rose and Lionel went to the store.
   N   C   N   V PR ADJ N

2. They wanted to buy some comic books with their money.
   P   V   ADJ ADJ N   P ADJ N

3. "Yikes!" cried Lionel. *X-Men* is on sale.
    I   V   N   N V P N

4. "I love *X-Men*, but *Spawn* is a great comic, too."
   P V   N   C   N   V   ADJ   N   ADJ

5. "*Spawn* and *X-Men* are both excellent."
    N   C   N   V ADJ   ADJ

✍ QUIZ #9 ✍
Subjects

Underline the subject in each of the following sentences.

1. <u>Amanda</u> stormed into the room.
2. (<u>You</u>) "Get away from my boyfriend!" (implied subject)
3. <u>He</u> is not your boyfriend.
4. <u>Amanda</u> picked up a chair and threw it at Jennifer.
5. Without a moment's hesitation, <u>Jennifer</u> ran out of the room

✍ QUIZ #10 ✍
Beverly Hills, Here We Come!

In the following passage, underline each verb and circle the subject that goes with it.

Thump. The (clubhouse) <u>landed</u> back in Babette's yard.

"(I) <u>am</u> glad (we)'<u>re</u> not cartoons any longer," (Sondra) <u>felt</u> her arms and legs, "(I) sure <u>didn't like</u> that feeling."

"Well, (we) <u>have had</u> a very exciting day so <u>far</u>, but (we) <u>have been</u> somewhat unlucky in our choices,"(Barnaby) <u>said</u>.

"Listen, guys, (you) just <u>don't know</u> how to pick nice, happy, fun places." (Bridget) <u>blew</u> a huge bubble, and <u>was lifted</u> off the ground a few inches. "Why <u>don't</u> (we) <u>go</u> and <u>visit</u> the Beverly Hillbillies? Now (there) <u>is</u> a bunch of friendly, down home folk. (Jethro) <u>is</u> dreamy. (Elly Mae) <u>is</u> sweet. (You) <u>Give</u> me that ticket."

(Bridget) <u>rubbed</u> the ticket while humming the theme song to *The Beverly Hillbillies*. The (clubhouse) <u>began</u> to shake once more.

✍ QUIZ #11 ✍
What's That in the Cement Pond? or Granny's Got a Gun!

Underline the subject and put parentheses around the predicate in each of the following sentences.

<u>The water</u> (began to bubble up around their feet.) <u>The clubhouse</u> (was barely floating.)

"<u>We</u>('ve landed in another swimming pool!") <u>Bridget</u> (wailed.) ("What are) <u>we</u> (going to do?")

("Well,) <u>we</u> (should probably get out of this clubhouse pronto,") <u>Barnaby</u> (suggested.)

<u>Jennifer</u> (peered out of the window.) "<u>I</u> (don't think that is a very good idea, Barnaby.")

("Why would) <u>you</u> (say that, Jennifer?) <u>We</u> (happen to be sinking.")

("Yeah, well) <u>I</u> (think) <u>I</u> (would rather drown.") <u>Jennifer</u> (pointed out of the window.)

"<u>Granny</u> (has got a gun!") <u>Bridget</u> (yelled.)

("What are) <u>you varmints</u> (doing in our ce-ment pond?") <u>Granny</u> (aimed the gun straight at the clubhouse.) "<u>You</u> (can tell me or tell my gun!")

("*Anna banana!*") <u>they all</u> (yelled at once.)

✍ QUIZ #12 ✍
Complete Sentences

Mark the complete sentences with an "S." Mark the fragments with an "F."

1. Granny marched into the room. S
2. After looking at the wreckage, left to find Jed. F
3. Sniffling and crying in the corner. F
4. Elly Mae was a mess. S
5. Jethro couldn't help but notice what a mess Elly Mae was. S

✍ QUIZ #13 ✍
Prepositional Phrases

Find the prepositional phrase or phrases in each sentence. Put parentheses around them.

1. (At the house), Sydney put some ice (on her nose.)
2. Jake, (in the kitchen), asked her if she wanted some soda.
3. The group (of them), Amanda, Sydney, and Jake, were pretty shaken up.
4. As always, Amanda felt triumphant (in her apartment).
5. Back (at the pool) Billy was getting ready (for a swim).

✍ QUIZ #14 ✍
Phrases and Clauses

Each of the following sentences has either a prepositional phrase or a dependent clause with the main, independent clause. Put parentheses around the phrases and underline the dependent clauses.

1. (After the party), Alison called Jane.
2. <u>Unless you were there</u>, you wouldn't believe it!
3. Jane called her sister <u>before she found out</u>.
4. Sydney told Jake (about the incident.)
5. <u>When he returned</u>, Billy spoke (to Amanda.)

✍ QUIZ #15 ✍
Compound Sentences

Rewrite each of these simple sentences as one compound sentence.

1. Amanda came home. She found Billy on her couch.
   Amanda came home and found Billy on her couch.
2. Billy told her to cool out. He would leave.
   Billy told her to cool out or he would leave.
3. I want to cool out! She won't let me!
   I want to cool out but she won't let me!

Now try rewriting these simple sentences as complex ones.

4. She ate pizza. It was her favorite food.
   She ate pizza because it was her favorite food.
5. She ate it every day. It was fattening.
   She ate it every day even though it was fattening.
6. She ate the pizza. She ate brownies.
   She ate the pizza and then she ate brownies.

Now turn the following complicated, confusing sentences into one or two simple sentences.

7. JuJu fruits, which are red, are the most nutritious.

   Red JuJu fruits are the most nutritious.

8. If you are going to San Francisco, which can be very foggy, make sure you bring your flashlight.

   If you are going to foggy San Francisco, make sure you bring your flashlight.

9. Eating hot dogs can be great, but Maria ate fifteen every day for lunch and soon began to feel sick about the whole thing.

   Eating hot dogs can be great. Maria ate fifteen every day for lunch, however, and began to feel sick about the whole thing.

✍ QUIZ #16 ✍
Putting it all Together

In the following sentences, circle the verbs, underline the subject, and put parentheses around the prepositional phrases. As well, mark "S" if it is a simple sentence, "C" if it is a compound sentence, and "X" if it is a complex sentence.

1. <u>Jennifer</u> (asked) Sondra what <u>it</u> (was) that <u>she</u> (wanted.) C

2. <u>I</u> (need) help! S

3. <u>Barnaby and Sondra</u> (offered to buy) Bridget some fresh bubble gum. S

4. (Do) <u>you</u> still (think) this <u>ticket</u>, even though <u>we</u> (ve had) some misadventures, (is) so bad? X

5. After <u>she</u> (thought) (about it), <u>Bridget</u> (was) convinced that her <u>friends</u> (were) right. X

6. Even though <u>we</u> (ve had) some problems, <u>I</u> still (think) this (could be) fun. C

7. (We) Let's go! S
8. We will all be together. S
9. We've had some bad luck, but we will try again. C

Singular and Plural Nouns

Change the singular nouns in parentheses to plural nouns.

1. Sondra asked Jennifer to eat fifteen bananas.

2. Taylor told me that his twelve monkeys escaped from their cages and wanted to wash their feet in the bath.

3. My favorite movies are comedies.

4. If you are going to put foxes in boxes, you'd better not bring them to churches or feed them lunches.

5. The shoemaker's elves put the shoes on the shelves all by themselves.

6. One of the great joys of eating burgers is that you don't need knives.

7. "Do you know where the ladies who sold me these shoes are?" asked Babette.

8. "I believe they are hiding in the bushes or behind that group of men." Taylor replied.

9. If you clear the dishes from the table, make sure you wrap the leftovers and put the bowls in the refrigerator.

10. If you take out the paints, wash the paintbrushes before you use them.

✍ QUIZ #18 ✍
Possessives

Fill in the missing parts of the following chart.

Singular	Singular possessive	Plural	Plural possessive
berry	berry's	berries	berries'
cat	cat's	cats	cats'
desk	desk's	desks	desks'
dog	dog's	dogs	dogs'
family	family's	families	families'
glove	glove's	gloves	gloves'
house	house's	houses	houses'
Jones	Jones's	Joneses	Joneses'
peach	peach's	peaches	peaches'
thief	thief's	thieves	thieves'

✍ QUIZ #19 ✍
Finding Direct and Indirect Objects

In each of the following sentences, circle the direct object and underline the indirect object (if one exists).

1. Dylan told <u>Brenda</u> the bad (news.)
2. Brenda sold <u>Tiffani</u> (rights) to the story.
3. The police asked <u>Dylan</u> several (questions.)
4. We wanted (bananas) and peeled (grapes) for the party.
5. Brandon ate ninety-eight (bananas) before winning the (contest.)

Identifying Predicate Nouns

Underline the predicate nouns in the following sentences.

1. Bart is an intrepid <u>explorer</u>.

2. Always afraid of his shadow, Mr. Burns is a <u>coward</u>.

3. That <u>kid</u> with the glasses is Milhouse.

4. Maggie is the youngest <u>child</u>.

5. Homer seems like a new <u>man</u>.

Babette Goes to Beverly Hills, Again

Underline the correct pronoun in each of the following sentences.

After returning from Beverly Hills, Barnaby looked at Babette. <u>He</u> wanted to know what <u>she</u> thought of that trip.

"Darling, that is not the real Beverly Hills, believe <u>me</u>. The real Beverly Hills is the place where you meet Brenda, Tiffani, Brandon, and Dylan. Let <u>us</u> go there," Babette cried.

"Do you think <u>we</u> really should try again?" Bridget wondered.

"<u>We</u> will never know the truth unless <u>we</u> try again!" Babette told <u>them</u>.

"Between you and <u>me</u>," Jennifer whispered to Bridget, "<u>I</u> don't care if <u>I</u> never see Beverly Hills again."

"Give <u>me</u> the ticket, darling." Babette rubbed. "Oh, Dylan, <u>I</u>, can't wait to meet you."

The clubhouse rumbled. Thwump! <u>They</u> landed in Dylan's yard.

"Who's there?" <u>they</u> heard a voice call from the kitchen.

✍ QUIZ #22 ✍
Relative Pronoun Time

Underline the correct relative pronoun in each of the following sentences.

1. Sideshow Bob, (<u>who,</u> whom) is Krusty's faithful sidekick, was after Bart.

2. *The Krusty the Clown Show*, (<u>which,</u> that) is Lisa's favorite, is on at 4 p.m. each day.

3. The Itchy and Scratchy episode, (<u>which,</u> that) Bart and Lisa like the best, is quite gory.

4. Could these be the children (who, <u>whom</u>) I brought into the world?

5. Maggie's favorite pacifier is the one (<u>that,</u> which) makes the most noise.

✍ QUIZ #23 ✍
Pronoun Agreement

Cross out the incorrect pronoun in each sentence and replace it with a better one.

1. Either Ginger or Mary Ann was sure to have brought <u>her</u> new bathing suit.

2. Anybody who has seen *Gilligan's Island* is certain to know that <u>he or she</u> has seen a classic.

3. "If anyone finds a way off this island, would <u>she or he</u> please let us know?" cried Mr. Howell.

4. "Oh, lovey," called Mrs. Howell, "neither Gilligan nor you is able to figure out what <u>he</u> really wants."

5. "All of <u>us</u> are happy as clams to be here. <u>We</u> want to stay on this island forever!" cried Mary Ann.

✍ QUIZ #24 ✍
Subject-Verb Agreement

Match the correct verb with the subject in the following sentences.

1. Alice *cooks* for the kids every night.

2. Every night, she *makes* their favorite meal: meatloaf.

3. *"Weren't* we going to have something different tonight, Alice?" *asks* Cindy.

4. "Yikes! Meatloaf again!" *cry* Jan and Marcia. "We need to watch our figures!"

5. *"Don't* you people have anything better to do than worry about dinner?" *wonders* Alice.

6. "Oh, no, not meatloaf!" *yells* Mr. or Mrs. Brady from upstairs.

7. "Oh, I *am* sick of trying to please all of you finicky Bradys!" Alice says as she *stomps* out of the house for the last time.

✍ QUIZ #25 ✍
Mr. Brady! Save us from Dylan!

Change all the present tense verbs that don't make sense to the past tense.

Dylan came into the yard and saw the clubhouse. The kids shook when they heard him yell and scream. "This club-house! Why did it land in my yard?"

Babette looked out of the window. "What a hunk!" she cried. "But he is being so violent. I am scared."

"Get out of here, or I'll call the police."

"Quick, give me the ticket. I have an idea," Taylor said. He rubbed the ticket and cried, "Help us, Mr. Brady!"

Suddenly, Mr. Brady walked into the yard. "Hey!" he yelled, "stop hitting that clubhouse!"

Dylan turned around. "This is my yard, man. I'll hit what I want."

"Excuse me, kids, but who lives here?"

"He does," Babette pointed sheepishly toward Dylan.

"Sorry, bud. My mistake." Mr. Brady picked up a stick and waved it at the house with Dylan. "Okay, you kids, get out of here or I'll have to call the police."

"Anna banana!" Taylor threw his hands up in disgust.

✍ QUIZ #26 ✍
Tenses

Fill in the correct verb form in each blank. The verb is in the infinitive form at the end of each sentence.

1. Yesterday, Barnaby *ate* twenty-seven chocolate chip cookies. (to eat)

2. Before he finished the cookies, he *had baked* four dozen. (to bake)

3. Right now, Bridget *chews* her favorite bubble gum. (to chew)

4. Tomorrow, Barnaby and Bridget *will go* to Jennifer's house. (to go)

5. By next Wednesday, Barnaby *will have baked* another 30 batches of chocolate chip cookies. (to bake)

✍ QUIZ #27 ✍
Correct Verb Forms

Underline the correct form of the verb in each sentence.

1. Max (<u>wept</u>, weeped) when he heard the bad news.

2. "My brother has been (hung, <u>hanged</u>)!" he cried.

3. "I have (laid, <u>lain</u>) on my bed too long!" he swore.

4. "If I had (slew, <u>slain</u>) that criminal, my poor brother would still be alive."

5. "I (brang, <u>brought</u>) this on myself," thought Max.

✍ QUIZ #28 ✍
Find the Participles

Put brackets around the participle phrases in the following sentences.

1. (Discovering his missing buffalo ribs), Fred called for Wilma.
2. (Using the information gathered in his research), Barney quickly figured out who the culprit was.
3. "This dish, (placed here by Wilma), has been tampered with!" cried Betty.
4. Bam Bam, (wishing to go out), yelled "Bam! Bam!"
5. Pebbles, (burping with some guilt), admitted to them all that she had eaten the ribs.

✍ QUIZ #29 ✍
Spotting Gerunds

Underline the gerunds in each of the following sentences.

1. I always liked <u>playing</u> baseball.
2. We all enjoyed <u>running</u> out onto the field.
3. <u>Batting</u> is the one thing I don't do that well.
4. <u>Fielding</u> is my area of expertise.
5. <u>Winning</u>, however, is something everybody likes.

✍ QUIZ #30 ✍
Infinitives

Spot the infinitive in each of the following sentences. For bonus points, say what part of speech it is.

1. Jethro wanted (to see) the sights in Beverly Hills.   N
2. (To go) to the races was Granny's favorite pastime.   N

3. Mr. Drysdale wanted (to eat) with the Clampetts.   N

4. Elly Mae hoped (to win) the beauty contest that week.   N

✑ QUIZ #31 ✑
Adjectives

Underline the correct adjective form in the following sentences.

1. Of all the kids, Barnaby was the <u>smartest</u>.

2. Taylor was <u>quieter</u> than Jennifer.

3. Instead of yummy mashed potatoes or healthy string beans, Bridget likes bubble gum <u>best</u>.

4. Between Sondra and Taylor, Sondra is the <u>odder</u>.

5. Babette is the <u>most</u> mysterious person you have ever met.

✑ QUIZ #32 ✑
Adjectives and Adverbs

Underline the correct word in each of the following sentences.

1. Amanda felt <u>well</u> on that <u>beautiful</u> day.

2. Jake wanted <u>badly</u> to call her and tell her how <u>sad</u> he felt.

3. Sydney told her sister that she dressed <u>well</u> for such a <u>good</u> day.

4. After coming to a <u>sudden</u> stop, Jake's <u>new</u> car screeched <u>loudly</u>.

5. Stomping <u>forcefully</u> out of the room, Amanda flipped her <u>thick</u> blonde hair from her <u>cool</u> eyes.

✍ QUIZ #33 ✍
Misplaced Modifiers

Underline the misplaced modifier, then rewrite each of the following sentences.

1. <u>Approaching his favorite TV star</u>, the Professor was right next to Barnaby.

   Approaching his favorite TV star, Barnaby stood next to the Professor.

2. <u>Meeting the voice of Wilma</u>, the set was filled with excitement for Sondra.

   Meeting the voice of Wilma, Sondra was filled with excitement.

3. <u>Going to the set of the TV show *Beverly Hills 90210*</u>, the ride was bumpy for Babette.

   The ride was bumpy for Babette as she went to the set of the TV show *Beverly Hills 90210*.

4. <u>Thinking about Amanda</u>, the pole hit a dreamy Jennifer smack in the face.

   Thinking about Amanda, a dreamy Jennifer hit a pole with her face.

✍ QUIZ #34 ✍
Preposition Time

Underline the correct preposition in each of the following sentences.

1. Tom went <u>to</u> Michael's Pet Store yesterday.

2. You know, Tom is really very different <u>from</u> Michael.

3. When Tom bought that fish <u>from</u> Michael, we were all very surprised.

4. <u>Besides</u> Tom, Michael doesn't have many friends.

5. <u>Between</u> Michael and Tom, Tom is the more friendly.

6. Tom was upset <u>with</u> Michael for selling him such a boring pet.

✍ QUIZ #35 ✍
Faulty Comparison

Correct the error in each of the following sentences.

1. "I love Mary Ann's smile so much more than Ginger!" cried Barnaby.

   "I love Mary Ann's smile so much more than Ginger's!" cried Barnaby.

2. "That may be true, but the story line on *Melrose Place* is far better than *Gilligan's Island*," shrieked Jennifer.

   "That may be true, but the story line on *Melrose Place* is far better than that of *Gilligan's Island*," shrieked Jennifer.

3. "The story line may be better, but Amanda's character is not nearly as nice as Mary Ann," answered Babette.

   "The story line may be better, but Amanda's character is not nearly as nice as Mary Ann's character," answered Babette.

4. "Amanda's dresses are far more stylish than Mary Ann," offered Taylor.

   "Amanda's dresses are far more stylish than those of Mary Ann," offered Taylor.

5. "Perhaps, but I still think that Mary Ann's hair is much prettier than Amanda," whispered Barnaby.

   "Perhaps, but I still think that Mary Ann's hair is much prettier than Amanda's," whispered Barnaby.

✍ QUIZ #36 ✍
Parallel Construction

Correct the error in each of the following sentences.

1. The castaways had tried many different ways to get off the island: <u>building rafts, signaling with flares, and to call ships with their radio.</u>

   building rafts, signaling with flares, and calling ships with their radio

2. Fred and Wilma were hosting the annual company picnic. They <u>fried brontosaurus burgers, grilled stegosaurus ribs, and were barbecuing as well.</u>

   They fried brontosaurus burgers, grilled stegosaurus ribs, and barbecued as well

3. Amanda wanted <u>to be successful, make a lot of money, and building a great empire.</u>

   to be successful, make a lot of money, and build a great empire

4. Warning: Watching too much television can <u>damage your brain, cause eyestrain, and may be interfering with your ability to read.</u>

   can damage your brain, cause eye strain, and interfere with your ability to read

5. <u>After eating, jumping rope, and to go swimming,</u> the gang went back to its clubhouse.

   After eating, jumping rope, and swimming

✍ QUIZ #37 ✍
Anna Banana, We're Home!

Punctuate the following paragraph. Remember that there is some flexibility here, but do your best and try to keep the paragraph clear.

Barnaby, Babette, Sondra, Taylor, and Jennifer were all quite tired but exhilarated nonetheless.

"The Professor was not quite as smart as I'd always hoped, but it was neat to finally see him anyway," Barnaby said.

"Maybe you're right about the Professor," said Jennifer, "but no one could compare to Amanda and her amazing clothes."

"Are you kidding? She was so mean," said Taylor.

"I think we all had some pretty exciting adventures," said Jennifer, "but I, for one, am happy to be back here. All that fighting and drama has worn me out."

"Yes," agreed Taylor. "I don't think I would really want to be in *The Brady Bunch* after all."

"I would definitely not want to be a part of that stupid Dylan's *Beverly Hills* show," said Babette. "I am very glad to be home."

The gang soon realized one thing—being part of a television show would be pretty exhausting after awhile.

"Let's burn that ticket," said Taylor. "It's the only safe, reasonable thing to do."

"I think he is right," said Barnaby. "Logically speaking, of course, we should cut our losses and just hang here despite the great heat."

They made a ceremonial fire and watched the silver ticket crumple and burn.

"There's no place like home!" cried Bridget.

✍ QUIZ #38 ✍
Diction

Underline the correct word in each of the following sentences.

1. After returning from her adventures, Bridget was so tired, she was barely <u>intelligible</u>.

2. We need to buy some paper from the <u>stationery</u> store and write all this down.

3. "<u>You're</u> kidding, right?" said Barnaby. "<u>It's</u> <u>too</u> unbelievable."

4. "That stupid ticket sure was <u>irritating</u>. We hardly had <u>any</u> good luck," growled Jennifer.

5. "If we had <u>fewer</u> adventures, we wouldn't have anything fun to talk about," Sondra pointed out.

6. "We should have <u>sneaked</u> past Dylan and gone to find Brandon," Babette pouted.

7. "Well, I am going to <u>lie</u> down now and take a nap. That was exhausting," Barnaby said.

✍ NOTES ✍

✍ NOTES ✍

✍ NOTES ✍

✎ NOTES ✎

✍ NOTES ✍

✍ NOTES ✍

NOTES

NOTES

✍ NOTES ✍

ABOUT THE AUTHOR

Liz Buffa joined the Princeton Review in 1989. She has taught classes in SAT, LSAT, GMAT and SAT-II special subject tests. She is a graduate of Wellesley College and lives in Locust Valley, N.Y. with her husband and two sons, David and Paul. This is her third book for the Princeton Review.

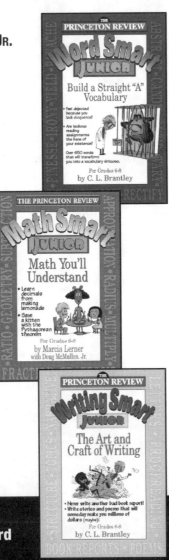